HOTSPOTS
BALI

Written by Alison Lemer with Jeroen van Marle
Original photography by Andy Day
Front cover photography by Schmid Reinhard/SIME-4Corners Images
Series design based on an original concept by Studio 183 Limited

Produced by Cambridge Publishing Management Limited
Project Editor: Alison Coupe
Layout: Donna Pedley
Maps: PCGraphics

Published by Thomas Cook Publishing
A division of Thomas Cook Tour Operations Limited
Company Registration No. 1450464 England
PO Box 227, Coningsby Road
Peterborough PE3 8SB, United Kingdom
email: books@thomascook.com
www.thomascookpublishing.com
+ 44 (0) 1733 416477

ISBN: 978-1-84157-814-9

First edition © 2007 Thomas Cook Publishing
Text © 2007 Thomas Cook Publishing
Maps © 2007 Thomas Cook Publishing
Project Editor: Diane Ashmore
Production/DTP Editor: Steven Collins

Printed and bound in Spain by GraphyCems

CONTENTS

WHAT'S IN YOUR GUIDEBOOK?

Independent authors Impartial, up-to-date information from our travel experts who meticulously source local knowledge.

Experience Thomas Cook's 165 years in the travel industry and guidebook publishing enriches every word with expertise you can trust.

Travel know-how Contributions by thousands of staff around the globe, each one living and breathing travel.

Editors Travel-publishing professionals, pulling everything together to craft a perfect blend of words, pictures, maps and design.

You, the traveller We deliver a practical, no-nonsense approach to information, geared to how you really use it.

● *Stunning beaches on Bali*

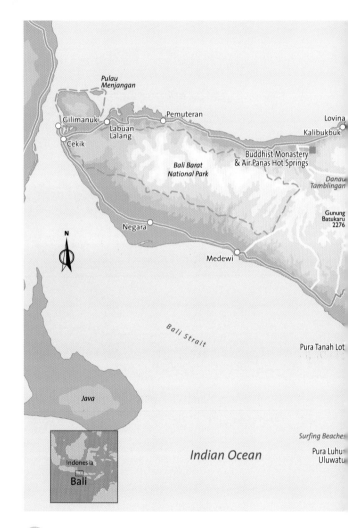

Pura Meduwe Karang

Kubutambahan

Singaraja

Bali Sea

Danau Buyan

Candikuning

Kintamani

Gunung Batur 1717

Danau Batur

Toya Bungkah

Tulamben

Danau Bratan

Pura Ulun Danu Bratan

Bedugul

Penelokan

Gunung Abang 2153

Amed

Botanical Gardens

Gunung Agung 3142

Jemeluk

Lipah Beach

Jatiluwih

Besakih

Culik

Bunutan

Aas

Royal Water Parks

Tampaksiring

Gunung Kawi

Tirtagangga

Amlapura

Bangli

Tenganan

Ubud

Bedulu

Klungkung

Candidasa

Pasir Putih

Tabanan

Goa Gajah

Mas

Yeh Pulu

Gianyar

Padangbai

Pura Goa Lawah

Lombok & Gili Islands

Batuan

Sukawati

Batubulan

Nusa Lembongan

Seminyak

DENPASAR

Jungutbatu

Sampalan

Legian

Sanur

Toyapakeh

Ped

Kuta

Nusa Ceningan

Lombok Strait

Ngurah Rai

Tanjung Benoa

Nusa Penida

Jimbaran

Bualu

Nusa Dua

Bukit Badung

Surfing Beaches

City
Large Town
Small Town
POI
Motorway
Main Road
Minor Road
Airport

Bali

0   10 km

0   5 miles

7

Getting to know Bali

This small, volcanic island has long been considered one of the jewels of Southeast Asia, fought over and conquered for much of its long history by outsiders from the neighbouring kingdoms of Java to the Dutch colonial occupation in the 19th and 20th centuries. Since the end of the World War II, it's been a province of the independent Republic of Indonesia, the world's largest Muslim nation, and despite the tragic terrorist bombings that hit Bali's largest resort in 2002, it's still far and away the most popular destination in the region. It's not hard to see why: its tropical location has blessed it with gorgeous weather, warm oceans, wide beaches, colourful coral reefs, brooding volcanoes and lush jungles – but Bali is just as famous for the friendliness and hospitality of its people, the vibrancy and beauty of its artistic and religious cultures, and the abundance of restaurants, nightlife, hotels and shopping, all available for budgets ranging from 'cheap as chips' to 'regal luxury'.

With an area of 5,632 sq km (2,175 sq miles) – it stretches only 140 km (87 miles) from east to west and 80 km (50 miles) from north to south – Bali is not a large island, and it's not difficult to take day trips all over the island or to try out a few different resorts. In the south are the most popular and most developed tourist areas, with the most attractive, golden-sand beaches and fantastic surf (to the west) or calm waters (to the east). Many visitors never bother straying from the southern resorts, but there's so much more that's worth seeing. Along the coasts in the east and north are a handful of smaller resorts, with fewer crowds, black-sand beaches and the island's best diving and snorkelling sites. Most of the western part of the island is taken up by Bali's only national park, Bali Barat, which covers 760 sq km (294 sq miles) of mountainous jungles. The central areas are arguably where you'll find the 'real' Bali – hard-working farmers on their terraced rice paddies, the temples (over 20,000 at last count) where the predominantly Hindu population worships its gods, and the cultural centres where Javanese-influenced performing and fine arts and handicrafts have flourished. And, of course, there are the massive inland volcanoes – the tallest, Gunung Agung, stands 3,142 m (10,308 ft) tall, and its cloud-ringed shape can be seen from just about anywhere on the island.

Even beyond Bali's amazing natural gifts, the easygoing pace and subtle charms of island life have worked their way with many a foreigner: Western expatriates have been drawn here for decades, and much of the tourist trade consists of repeat visitors. So don't be surprised if you find yourself dreaming of returning to Bali long after your trip has ended.

⏺ *Stone carvings are used to decorate temples and palaces on Bali*

THE BEST OF BALI

No matter what kind of holiday you're after, you can find it on Bali – surfing and diving in warm tropical waters, getting pampered at a spa, dancing all night, experiencing traditional arts and cultures, indulging in inexpensive dining and shopping, or even just lazing on a beach with a cold beer. Fortunately, the island is small enough that you can easily make trips to see it all.

TOP 10 ATTRACTIONS

- **Kuta** The most famous – and infamous – area on the island, packed with shops, restaurants, bars, nightclubs and partying tourists. Sunbathers and surfers will love its broad beach (see page 14).

- **Ubud** At this inland town you'll find traditional Balinese arts, crafts and culture, a wide range of recreational adventure activities and great restaurants, shops and spas (see page 68).

- **Pulau Menjangan** The coral reefs surrounding this tiny island off the northwest coast are some of the best diving and snorkelling sites in Bali (see page 61).

- **Pura Tanah Lot** One of Bali's most sacred temples, famous for its striking location on a rocky, wave-lashed outcrop off the southwestern coast – especially stunning at sunset (see page 75).

- **Delicious seafood** For only a few rupiah (Bali currency) you can get some of the freshest seafood you've ever had, caught that morning and grilled to order at the *warungs* (food stalls or cafés) on Jimbaran beach (see page 24).

- **Tirtagangga** A regal water park with graceful pools and fountains built by one of the last kings of Bali (see page 78).

- **Lovina** A quiet resort on the north coast that's a good base for divers or anyone wanting to get away from the crowds for a bit (see page 55).

- **Nusa Lembongan** This small island in the southeast has beautiful cove beaches and some fantastic surfing and diving spots (see page 47).

- **The Gili Islands** Three tiny islands off the coast of neighbouring Lombok that are ideal for sunbathing, diving, snorkelling and whiling away warm nights by the water's edge (see page 85).

- **Gunung Kawi** These huge memorial shrines, almost a thousand years old, were hand-carved into the cliffs of a peaceful river valley (see page 72).

◆ *Sunrise over Lovina*

SYMBOLS KEY

The following symbols are used throughout this book:

@ address   ☎ telephone   ⓕ fax   ⓦ website address   ⓔ email

🕐 opening times   ⓘ important

The following symbols are used on the maps:

ℹ️	information office	○	city
✉️	post office	○	large town
🛍️	shopping	○	small town
✈️	airport	■	poi (point of interest)
✚	hospital	=	motorway
🛡️	police station	—	main road
🚌	bus station		minor road
🚆	railway station	—	railway
✝️	church		

❶ numbers denote featured cafés, restaurants & evening venues

RESTAURANT CATEGORIES

The symbol after the name of each restaurant listed in this guide indicates the price of a typical three-course meal without drinks for one person:

£ under Rp50,000

££ Rp50,000–150,000

£££ Rp150,000 and over

⊙ *Picture yourself watching the calm ocean*

RESORTS
Places under the sun

Kuta & around

By far the biggest and most popular tourist resort on Bali, conveniently located just north of the airport, is the area known as Kuta – actually a large conurbation consisting of the once separate villages of **Kuta** (to the south), **Legian** (in the middle) and **Seminyak** (to the north). Kuta is a bustling, hedonistic place, packed with hotels, shops, restaurants, bars and nightclubs designed to cater to any taste or budget, not to mention plenty of international tourists – one of the least traditionally Balinese places in Bali.

🔺 *There are plenty of places to surf in Bali*

That said, there are still plenty of reasons to enjoy Kuta. The broad, pleasant beach is justly famous for its great surfing and its gorgeous sunsets, and the options for dining, drinking and shopping seem almost infinite; while it may be lacking in attractions such as museums or temples, just walking around window-shopping and enjoying the streetlife is a sight in itself. Legian still has plenty of shops but is considered a bit quieter than Kuta, with fewer backpackers and more families, while laid-back Seminyak is home to many expats and has the poshest, most sophisticated restaurants, bars and nightclubs.

◓ *The colourful Barong face at Kuta Temple*

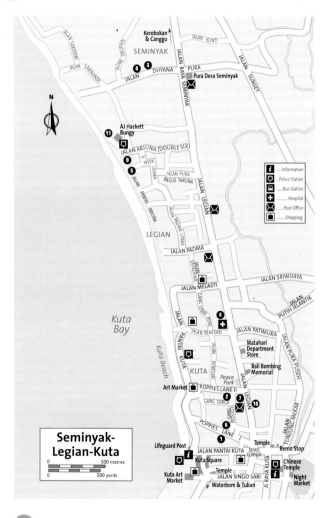

It's a spread-out area, but not difficult to navigate. There are two north–south roads, Jalan Pantai Kuta, running parallel to the beach, and Jalan Legian, about 500 m ($\frac{1}{3}$ mile) to the east. (Main roads are generally named after their village, and Jalan Legian eventually turns into Jalan Raya Seminyak.) Other roads and *gangs* (alleyways or narrow streets) run parallel or perpendicular in between them. To the south of Kuta is the small area of **Tuban**; to the north, Seminyak blends into **Petitenget**, followed by **Kerobokan** and **Canggu**, areas that have become popular with expats and return visitors (Kerobokan in particular is becoming known for some fine restaurants along its main road).

Kuta is only 10–15 minutes from the airport by taxi. The streets of the area are always choked with traffic and befuddled by a series of one-way regulations, so don't bother renting a car here unless you're planning to take a day trip elsewhere. Most people walk, hire *ojeks* (motorcycle taxis) or take taxis to get around.

BEACHES

One of the Kuta area's main attractions is its famous white-sand beach that stretches for 8 km (5 miles) along the coast. Even in low season it's abuzz with activity – with hawkers selling souvenirs or offering manicures and hair-plaiting, vendors selling snacks or renting out umbrellas and loungers, surfers riding the waves, tourist families, young backpackers, joggers and their dogs – and yet it's still quite clean and pleasant for strolling. The hawkers generally stay under the long row of shade trees by the road, so once you walk past them they shouldn't bother you much.

Kuta is really better for surfing than swimming, due to the constant waves and the strong undertow, but if you do go for a dip, read the warning signs and stick between the striped red-and-yellow flags. There are a number of lifeguard stations, but despite this around a dozen people per year drown here. Advanced surfers looking for more of a challenge can try **Berewa Beach** in Canggu.

THINGS TO SEE & DO

Bali bombing memorial

This small plaza has a beautifully carved wall with a memorial listing
the names of the two hundred people killed when terrorists set off a
massive car bomb on this site in 2002. Across the street is Peace Park,
a small grassy area where a popular nightclub, one of the bombers'
targets, once stood.

ⓐ Jl Legian, Kuta

Horse riding

The **Umalas Stables and Equestrian Resort**, located just north of
Seminyak, has 30 horses and offers lessons as well as group rides
along the beach or through rice paddies.

ⓐ Jl Lestari 9X, Kerobokan ⓣ (0361) 731 402 ⓦ www.balionhorse.com

🔺 *There's more than one way to get around Bali*

Night market

The cheapest dinners in Kuta can be found at the *pasar senggol* (night market), filled with numerous street vendors and *warungs*. For only a few thousand rupiah, you can get a filling Indonesian meal such as *nasi goreng* (see page 92), *soto ayam* (see page 92) or barbecued fresh fish, accompanied by a cold *Bintang*.

ⓐ Jalan Blambangan, Kuta

Shopping

You can find shops pretty much everywhere in Kuta, but the main areas are along Jalan Legian and **Kuta Square**, just south of the beach road. This small plaza has mostly Western outlets – Quiksilver, Rip Curl, D&G, Levi's – as well as the large Matahari department store and supermarket (see Shopping, page 94). Just south of Kuta Square is the main *pasar seni* (art market), filled with endless stalls selling paintings, handicrafts, souvenirs and clothing.

DEALING WITH HAWKERS

You'll find hawkers and touts, with their constant refrains of offers for transport, souvenirs, food and services, at pretty much every resort except Nusa Dua, but especially in the area around Kuta and its beach. As annoying as it can get, remember that most Western visitors are incredibly wealthy by local standards, and these people are really just trying to earn a living – it's important to keep your temper in check. The best way to handle it is simply say 'No, thank you' firmly and politely and keep walking. If you say 'Maybe later', they'll remember you and bother you even more if you pass them again. And definitely don't start bargaining unless you're interested in buying – if they accept an offer you make, you'll be obligated to follow through with the deal.

◗ The ubiquitous hawker

Surfing

Bali's original spot for surfing is Kuta Beach – an American hotelier introduced the sport here in the 1930s. The tube waves are quite uniform and consistent, and with no coral or rocks and a nice sand beach, it's a great place for beginners to learn without fear of wiping out. The greatest concentration of surf schools and gear stores can be found in Kuta and Legian, too.

Bali Learn to Surf ⓐ Hard Rock Hotel, Jl Pantai Kuta, Kuta ⓣ (0361) 761 869 ext. 8816 ⓦ www.balilearntosurf.com

Bali Surf School ⓐ Jl Arjuna/Double Six 7A, Legian ⓣ (0361) 733 666

Ripcurl School of Surf ⓐ Jl Arjuna/Double Six, Legian ⓣ (0361) 735 858 ⓦ www.schoolofsurf.com

Water park

The large **Waterbom** water park is only a few minutes' walk south of Kuta Square. It's a fun family visit on a hot day, with all kinds of water rides and slides (built to international safety standards), sporting activities, swimming pools, a supervised children's area, restaurants and lifeguards on duty at all times. There's even retail shopping and a massage spa for adults.

ⓐ Jl Kartika Plaza, Tuban ⓣ (0361) 755 676
ⓦ www.waterbom.com ⓒ 09.00–18.00

TAKING A BREAK

Cafés
Fat Yogi's £ ❶

A large menu of standard fare – Indonesian dishes, pizzas and pasta, burgers, chicken and fish, etc. – in an airy setting on two levels.
ⓐ Poppies Lane I, Kuta ⓣ (0361) 751 665

Warung Indonesia £ ❷

Great little *warung* with Indonesian food from as cheap as Rp7,000. Try the *nasi goreng* or *soto ayam*, or create your own mixed plate. A number of vegetarian options, too. ⓐ Gang Ronta, Kuta

Warung Kita £ ❸

Small but clean and comfortable café with buffet-style Indonesian food – assemble your own *campur* (mixed) plate from the vegetable and meat offerings, or order *à la carte* from the Indonesian and Western menus. ⓐ Jl Dhyana Pura/Abimanyu 103, Seminyak

AFTER DARK

Restaurants, bars & nightclubs
Aromas Café ££ ❹

One of Kuta's best vegetarian restaurants, with very tasty fresh juices, large salads and an international selection of mains, including Indonesian, Greek, Lebanese and Indian dishes. There's an informal café at the front and a larger dining area in the back. ⓐ Jl Legian, Kuta ❶ (0361) 751 003

Lanai Beachbar & Grille ££ ❺

Subdued but sophisticated, this beach-road restaurant offers beautiful ocean views from its upper-deck dining area. An upscale menu features internationally-influenced mains like Moroccan lamb stew or sesame duck confit. The wine and cocktail list is extensive, so it's a good place just for drinks, too. ⓐ Jl Pantai Arjuna/Double Six, Legian ❶ (0361) 731 305

TJ's Mexican Restaurant ££ ❻

Considered by many to have the best Mexican food in Bali, with large portions, great margaritas and a pleasant setting with a small water garden. A Kuta institution since 1984. ⓐ Poppies Lane I, Kuta ❶ (0361) 751 093

Maccaroni Club £££ ❼

Milano-style and very chic lounge-restaurant with three levels, authentic Italian food and live or DJed music nightly, with great cocktails and an international wine list. Free wi-fi and internet terminals upstairs. ⓐ Jl Legian 52, Kuta ❶ (0361) 754 662 ⓦ www.maccaroniclub.com

Bahiana ⓼

Salsa bar with all sorts of Latin music – samba, merengue, Latin jazz, etc. – as well as Cuban- and South-American-style cocktails and weekly theme parties. ⓐ Jl Dhyana Pura/Abimanyu 4, Seminyak ⓣ (0361) 738 662 ⓦ www.bahiana-bali.com ⓛ 17.00–late

De Ja Vu ⓽

A sleek, cosmpolitan lounge on the beach road with subdued polychromatic lighting and huge windows, perfect for cocktails at sunset. DJs play jazz and lounge music nightly. ⓐ Jl Pantai Arjuna/Double Six, Legian ⓣ (0361) 732 777 ⓛ 16.00–04.00

Double Six ('66') ⓾

So well known, it renamed a street. Stylish and sophisticated, this late-night club on the beach lets you dance till dawn, with international DJs spinning the latest tunes. Really gets going around 02.00.
ⓐ Jl Pantai Arjuna/Double Six 66, Legian ⓣ (0361) 731 266
ⓦ www.doublesixclub.com ⓛ 23.00–06.00

Jimbaran & the Bukit Badung

Bali's arid southern peninsula, known as the Bukit ('hill'), has some of Bali's nicest beaches, most expensive resort hotels and tall, rugged cliffs. The west coast features the fishing village of Jimbaran Bay and some fantastic surfing spots, as well as a popular temple with breathtaking views. Located just south of the airport, Jimbaran and the Bukit are most easily accessed by a quick taxi trip or with your own transport, as *bemo* (minibus or van) service is limited and discontinues in the afternoon.

BEACHES

The beach at Jimbaran is a long crescent of soft, yellow sand, with numerous seafood *warungs* (see page 26) and a string of exclusive, five-star hotels, located mostly at the southern end. Facilities are limited, but

⬥ *Sunset over Jimbaran beach*

it's a nice, quiet alternative to Kuta beach, offering the same amazing sunsets. The water's calm enough for swimming (although there are no lifeguards), and if the weather's clear you can see Bali's volcanoes off in the distance to the north. See page 26 for more on surfing beaches.

THINGS TO SEE & DO

Pura Luhur Uluwatu

This cliff-top temple is one of the island's most sacred, meant to protect Bali from evil spirits from the southwest. It's certainly one of its most beautiful temple settings, sitting almost 100 m (328 ft) above the ocean, which crashes dramatically into the rocks below; once you've seen the temple, walk down the side road to the left for an even better vista. At sunset the views are incredible, and the crowds larger to match. Uluwatu

⏶ *The sacred cliff-top temple of Pura Luhur Uluwatu*

is also known for its resident band of wild monkeys, which you can feed (from a distance!) with bags of peanuts sold there.

🕐 daylight hours ❶ Admission charge; sarong and sash rental

Seafood warungs

The main attraction at Jimbaran is the numerous beachside *warungs* serving the morning's fresh catches, courtesy of the well-known fish market up at the north end. They're situated in three areas down the beach: at the north end, in the middle and at the south end – the ones up north are generally the cheapest (and cheapest-looking) – with rows of tables lined down towards the ocean and big BBQ grills set up for cooking. Pick your fresh seafood (fish, lobster, prawns, crabs, squid, etc.) from an ice bucket; it's weighed and charged per 100 g ($3\frac{1}{2}$ oz), then grilled over a fire of coconut husks with various sauces, herbs and spices, and accompanied by generous portions of rice, vegetables and potatoes (so at least vegetarians won't starve). Many are open for lunch but the crowds get liveliest at night, when the gorgeous tropical sunset offers the perfect backdrop for dinner.

Surfing beaches

Running along the coast south of Jimbaran Bay are some of Bali's best surfing beaches, with the evocatively named Dreamland and the Impossibles, as well as Balangan, Bingin, Padang Padang, Suluban and Uluwatu (near the temple). The consistent breaks and left-handers (at their best from April to October) offer thrilling challenges for advanced surfers, but these waves are too rough for beginners, who should stick to Kuta. Nor are the waves good for swimming or sunbathing, although they're certainly beautiful for the view or to watch the daring folk on the boards. From the main road to Uluwatu, look for access-road signs to the beaches; some will have small road tolls or parking fees. Be aware that many also have steep access stairs down the cliff.

TAKING A BREAK

Cafés

If you love seafood, head for Jimbaran beach. Otherwise, there's not much around except hotel cafés and some *warungs* along the main road, Jalan Raya Uluwatu.

AFTER DARK

Restaurants

The inexpensive seafood *warungs* do a brisk dinner trade, but if you want something more upmarket, there are a number of fine restaurants attached to the five-star resorts and hotels found towards the southern end of the bay.

Nelayan £££

Romantic beachside dining (some tables are right on the sand) with French-Mediterranean cuisine and special lobster menus. ⓐ Jimbaran Puri Bali hotel, Jl Yoga Perkanti ☎ (0361) 701 605 ⓦ www.jimbaranpuribali.com ⏰ 11.00–17.00, 18.00–22.30

PJ's £££

Open-air dining on a beachfront deck – unbeatable at sunset – featuring fresh seafood dishes and gourmet Mediterranean and Italian cuisine. ⓐ Four Seasons Resort, Jl Bukit Permai ☎ (0361) 701 010 ⓦ www.fourseasons.com/jimbaranbay ⏰ 11.00–22.00 ❶ Reservations recommended

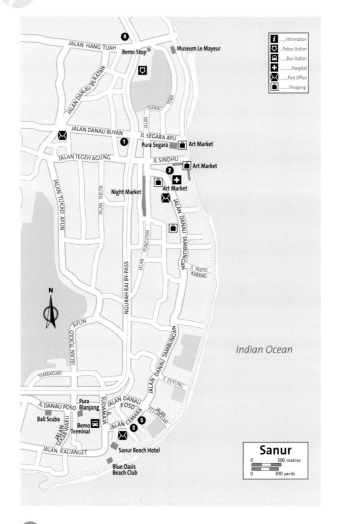

Sanur

| 0 | 300 metres |
| 0 | 300 yards |

Sanur

A lovely town east of Denpasar and within day trip-reach of most destinations on Bali, Sanur is known for its long white-sand beach with relatively little hassle from vendors, and where children can play safely in the shallows without fear of big waves. Often called a more family-friendly version of Kuta, and sometimes dismissed as boring, Sanur actually has a lot going for it and even has some good nightlife options. The best thing about it is perhaps its relaxed village-like atmosphere and the relative lack of huge resort hotels. In the evenings, when it cools down, join the locals when they come out to the beach to scamper on the sand, paddle in the water and munch on hot snacks. Sanur is not just about lazing around and visiting spas; indeed, it offers many watersports options, and if you like being dragged along on a big banana, pulled into the air on an inflatable wing or dunked in the water on a diving or surfing course, you'll love it here. The snorkelling off Sanur beach is not very good, so if you want to see any signs of aquatic life you need to sail out to the various dive sites with a boatman or one of the diving companies. After all the action, the shopping's pretty good and fairly concentrated along a few roads, and you can feed your brain with visits to the famous art museum or on trips to one of many dance performances in and around town. Sanur is a popular place for expats to live, and as a result there's quite a sophisticated restaurant scene with a good variety of cuisines. At night, there are plenty of lively bars along the beach and inland along the town's main roads, though you'll have to go to Kuta for proper clubbing.

Sanur is quickly reached by taxi from Kuta and Denpasar, or by one of Perama's tourist buses.

BEACHES

Sanur's 5km (3 miles) of wide, white-sand beach is great for sunbathing or strolling in the shade of trees – unlike Kuta there's no road behind the beach. The busiest part is in the north near the high-rise Inna Grand hotel.

⬥ *A colourful fishing boat on Sanur's shore*

THINGS TO SEE & DO

Dance shows

See a traditional *kecak* or *barong* dance show in a local hotel or restaurant, or visit one of the dance stages in and around town with their daily performances.

Museum Le Mayeur

This attractive Balinese house along the beach in northern Sanur was the home of Belgian artist Adrien Jean Le Mayeur de Merpes (1880–1958), who married the beautiful dancer Ni Polok when she was 15 (while he was over 50). Who can blame him? She looks dazzling on the many paintings in the museum.

🅐 Jl Hang Tuah 🕔 08.00–15.00 Sun–Thur, 08.00–13.00 Fri, closed Sat

Bali Scuba

One of several top-class and often foreign-run diving outfits in Sanur, despite the lack of good coral near the resort. PADI courses, beginners' dives, snorkelling trips and more.

🅐 Jl Danau Poso 40 ☎ (0361) 288 610 🅦 www.baliscuba.com
🕔 07.00–18.00

Blue Oasis Beach Club

A watersports centre in southern Sanur offering everything from kitesurfing and kayaking to waterskiing and surfing. High standards of safety and professionalism.

🅐 Jl Danau Tamblingan, Sanur Beach Hotel ☎ (0361) 288 011
🅦 www.blueoasisbeachclub.com 🕔 08.00–21.00

TAKING A BREAK

Cafés

Plenty of good cafés and restaurants catering to expats and travellers can be found along Jalan Danau Tamblingan, running parallel to the beach.

Splash Bakery £ ❶
Delicious fresh bread, cakes and other baked products to eat in or for take-away. ❷ Jl Bypass Ngurah Rai ❶ (0361) 288 186 ❷ 08.00–20.00

Warung Bento £ ❷
A simple bamboo-clad restaurant serving a combination of well-priced Japanese *bentos* (lunch boxes) and local Javanese food. ❷ Jl Danau Tamblingan 27 ❶ (0361) 282 572 ❷ 10.00–22.00

🔺 *Relax under the shade of a Frangipani tree on Sanur beach*

AFTER DARK

Restaurants & bars

Sanur's nightlife starts late; don't expect any action before 23.00. Though there aren't any good clubs, there are many bars with live music that stay open till late. For a concentration of friendly local bars, head for Jalan Hang Tuah in north Sanur.

The Cat and Fiddle ££ ❸

Popular with both expats and travellers, this English pub has all the food and drink favourites including fish and chips, shepherd's pie and lager on tap. Live Irish music every Tuesday. ⓐ Jl Mertasari
ⓣ (0361) 270 572 ⓛ 11.00–23.00

Kafe Wayang ££ ❹

A great restaurant for either lunch or dinner, and also gets lively at night when the live band climbs on stage; it hosts popular jam sessions on Fridays. ⓐ Jl Bypass Ngurah Rai, Komplek Sanur Raya 12–14
ⓣ (0361) 287 591 ⓛ 12.00–02.00

Mezzanine £££ ❺

Excellent Thai food served in posh surroundings, and livened up with live music later on at night. ⓐ Jl Mertasari, Puri Santrian Hotel
ⓣ (0361) 270 624 ⓛ 12.00–02.00, kitchen closes at 23.00

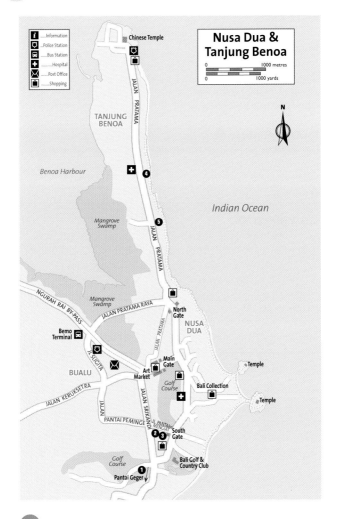

Nusa Dua & Tanjung Benoa

On the eastern side of the Bukit peninsula is the exclusive beach resort Nusa Dua, filled with luxury resort hotels with a full range of activities and facilities designed to pamper and please. Tanjung Benoa, its slightly less upmarket cousin to the north, developed its own hotels and restaurants but thankfully left its small village alone. Outside the gates of Nusa Dua is the village of **Bualu**, home to many of the hotels' employees, which has an art market and some mid-range restaurants.

Taxis or private transport are the best ways to travel to and from or around Nusa Dua, as *bemo* service here is limited to nonexistent. Many of the hotels and some of the restaurants here offer free shuttle service and pick-ups around the area.

BEACHES

Nusa Dua's long white-sand beach is the stuff of vacation brochures, and the paved promenade that stretches alongside for 5 km (3 miles) makes for a pleasant stroll. The water is fine for swimming, except at low tide when the reef is exposed. Just behind the shopping centre, the coast juts out into two small headlands ('Nusa Dua' means 'two islands'), each with some shade trees and a small temple – nice for a picnic. Conversely, **Tanjung Benoa**'s beach is not terribly appealing – it's primarily for watersports and not worthwhile for sunbathing or swimming.

Pantai Geger

South of the golf course is this clean, white-sand *pantai* (beach) with calm surf and safe swimming. It's popular with expats and tourists, especially with families. No lifeguards or shops, but there are a few beach vendors, sunshades for hire and a popular restaurant with a Western-friendly menu. Access is via a narrow road south of The Balé villas; vehicles can be driven almost down to the beach and there's easy parking available.

THINGS TO SEE & DO

Birdwatching
A left turn out of Nusa Dua's North Gate eventually brings you to a large mangrove swamp – also home to the Nusa Dua sewage works, but don't let that throw you – with a picturesque lagoon, where you can see flocks of kingfishers, herons and other water-loving birds. Early mornings are the best time.

Chinese temple
The village of Tanjung Benoa was traditionally a trading port, and you can see evidence of its multicultural influences at its northern tip, where a Hindu temple, a mosque and a Chinese Buddhist temple sit within a few blocks of each other. The Chinese community here is one of the oldest on Bali: their merchant ancestors are believed to have migrated here in the 8th century.

ⓐ Jl Segara Ening, Tanjung Benoa

◓ *White-sand beach at Nusa Dua*

Golf course

The 18 hole course at the **Bali Golf and Country Club** has been called one of the best in Asia, and with three types of terrain and beautiful mountain and ocean views, it's certainly one of the prettiest. Facilities include a spa, equipment hire and a restaurant.

ⓐ Nusa Dua ☎ (0361) 771 791 Ⓦ www.baligolfandcountryclub.com

Shopping centre

Bali Collection is a large, open-air shopping centre in the middle of Nusa Dua, with Western brands like Dolce & Gabbana and Quiksilver, as well as local shops, a SOGO department store, supermarket and international restaurants. Starbucks? Of course.

ⓐ Jl Pratama, Nusa Dua ☎ (0361) 771 662 Ⓦ www.bali-collection.com

Pura Luhur Uluwatu

See Jimbaran and the Bukit Badung, page 24.

Watersports

Tanjung Benoa's calm waters are great for watersports, and its main road, Jalan Pratama, is lined with operators offering parasailing, jet-skiing, waterskiing, wake boarding, speed or glass-bottom boat rides, and the new 'flying fish'.

Benoa Marine Recreation ☎ (0361) 771 757 Ⓦ www.bmrbali.com
Rai Watersports ☎ (0361) 733 815
YOS Marine Adventures ☎ (0361) 775 438 Ⓦ www.yosdive.com

TAKING A BREAK

Cafés

There are some inexpensive *warungs* on Jalan Srikandi in Bualu or Jalan Pratama in Tanjung Benoa. Jalan Pantai Mengiat, just outside Nusa Dua's South Gate, has some mid-range tourist restaurants.

Nusa Dua Beach Grill ££ ❶

Casual beach restaurant with salads, seafood and great smoothies.
ⓐ Pantai Geger ❶ (0361) 743 4779

AFTER DARK

Restaurants

The best restaurants here are generally found at the luxury hotels,
although there are others along Jalan Pratama and outside the Nusa
Dua gates.

Poco Loco ££ ❷

Local branch of Kuta's colourful Mexican restaurant, with large portions,
great fajitas, frozen margaritas and live music. ⓐ Jl Pantai Mengiat 12,
Bualu ❶ (0361) 773 923 ● 18.00–00.00

Ulam ££ ❸

A popular seafood restaurant just outside Nusa Dua's South Gate, with
large combination baskets and succulent lobster, crab and grilled fish
dishes. ⓐ Jl Pantai Mengiat 14, Bualu ❶ (0361) 771 590

Bumbu Bali £££ ❹

One of Bali's finest restaurants, serving classic Balinese cuisine (with
plenty of vegetarian dishes) from expat chef Heinz von Holzen, whose
multi-course *rijsttafels* (see page 93) are a particular speciality. *Legong*
dances are staged on Wednesday and Friday nights, and the thrice-
weekly cookery classes are very popular (see website). ⓐ Jl Pratama,
Tanjung Benoa ❶ (0361) 774 502 ⓦ www.balifoods.com ● 11.00–23.00
❶ Classes require 2-day advance booking

Spice £££ ❺

Modern pan-Asian cuisine showcasing a variety of Eastern spices in an
elegant setting with ocean views. ⓐ Conrad Bali Resort, Jl Pratama, Tanjung
Benoa ❶ (0361) 778 788 ● 18.00–23.00 ❶ Reservations recommended

Candidasa

This relaxed little resort is a good base if you want something quieter and further afield than the southern resorts, or for exploring more of the eastern region, especially its notable diving sites. Most of Candidasa's restaurants, hotels and shops are lined up along either side of the main road, Jalan Raya Candidasa, although some facilities may be limited – on our visit the closest ATMs were 10 km (6 miles) away in either Padangbai (see page 44) or Amlapura, the district capital.

BEACHES

Alas, Candidasa's beach – or rather its lack of one – is a living fable about the dangers of overdevelopment. In the 1980s, the tourist boom led to the construction of huge tourist facilities in the south, and the coral reefs off Candidasa's shore were harvested to make lime for cement; unfortunately, it left the lovely yellow-sand beach so exposed to the ocean that much of it just washed away. Concrete jetties have protected some remaining patches, including one by the large, placid, lotus-strewn **lagoon** at the eastern end of town and another at the western end of the main road.

Pasir Putih

If you're feeling particularly adventurous, head for this picturesque, undeveloped white-sand beach about 5 km (3 miles) east of Candidasa. Take the main road towards Amlapura to the village of Perasi and look for the turn-off, a narrow road amongst a row of shops; ask a local if you can't find it. (If you get as far as the petrol station, you've gone too far.) Follow the paved road, pay the toll (a few thousand rupiah), and then drive for about ten minutes down a rutted dirt track to the beach. (If you don't have a sturdy vehicle, park at the small temple 1 km (²/₃ mile) past the toll and walk from there.)

You'll see more fishing boats than tourists at this beach; in fact, there's a good chance you'll be the only ones there. There are no real

◔ *The lagoon at Candidasa*

facilities (including public toilets) other than a few stands selling cheap Indonesian food and beer. There are also no lifeguards, so be careful swimming as there are some strong currents if you go too far from shore.

THINGS TO SEE & DO

Diving
There are some spectacular wall dives, including Tepekong Canyon, near the three tiny islands just offshore, but they're only for advanced divers. There are also some snorkelling spots: enquire at one of the dive centres, most of which also offer trips to other sites at Padangbai, Nusa Penida and Nusa Lembongan (see page 47), and Amed and Tulamben (see pages 51–3)

Dive Lite ⓐ Jl Raya Candidasa ⓣ (0363) 416 60 ⓦ www.divelite.com
Sub Ocean Bali ⓐ Jl Sengkidu ⓣ (0363) 414 11 ⓦ www.suboceanbali.com
YOS Marine Adventures ⓐ at Asmara hotel, Jl Raya Candidasa
ⓣ (0363) 419 29 ⓦ www.yosdive.com

Tenganan
The nearby village of Tenganan is one of the few *Bali Aga* (original Balinese) communities on the island. They rejected the sweeping social and religious changes brought over by the Hindu Majapahit kindgom of Java when it conquered Bali in the 14th century, and instead adhere to the traditional animist religion (Animism) and original social structures of pre-Hindu Bali. Tenganan artisans are famous for their double-*ikat* cloth (see Shopping, page 94), fine baskets and traditional manuscripts and calendars etched onto dried *lontar* palm leaves.
ⓐ About 3.5 km (2 miles) north of Candidasa ⓒ Daylight hours
ⓘ Admission by donation

TAKING A BREAK

Cafés
All the options in town are lined up along Jalan Raya Candidasa, so it's easy simply to stroll until you find something that looks good.

Queen's Café £
Standard options at good prices, especially the three-course set menus. Live music weekly. ⓐ Jl Raya Candidasa ⓣ (0363) 416 55

🔺 *Tenganan woman weaving double-ikat cloth*

AFTER DARK

Restaurants & bars

There are a quite few excellent restaurants here, especially attached to the nicer hotels, but not much nightlife to speak of. Most places shut by 23.00.

Legend Rock Café £

A café serving Western and Indonesian food with a bar and live music several nights a week. ⓐ Jl Raya Candidasa ⓣ (0361) 416 36

Mr. Grumpy's £

Sports café with a large-screen TV, satellite channels, DVD library, and old sitcoms and films shown daily. There's also a billiards table, beer and wine, and a simple bar menu. ⓐ Jl Raya Candidasa ⓛ to 23.00 daily

Kedai ££

An Asian-fusion menu with an emphasis on seafood, plus a popular multi-course tasting menu, modern décor and an ocean view. ⓐ Jl Raya Candidasa ⓣ (0361) 420 20 ⓦ www.dekco.com/Kedai ⓛ 10.30–22.30 daily

Vincent's ££

A laid-back, cosmopolitan place, with classic jazz, a European and Balinese menu with vegetarian options and an international wine list. ⓐ Jl Raya Candidasa ⓣ (0363) 413 68 ⓦ www.vincentsbali.com ⓛ 12.00–22.00 daily

Padangbai

Sleepy Padangbai, on the east coast just south of Candidasa, is a pleasant small town with a ferry harbour and a well-tended beachfront street with guesthouses and restaurants. With just a handful of drinking options it's certainly no party destination, but the white-sand beaches and the snorkelling and diving are well worth the trip. Padangbai is very quiet except for the flurry of activity every 90 minutes or so when a ferry from Lombok or Nusa Penida steams into port, releasing a stream of traffic.

Padangbai is easily reached from Kuta or Ubud by Perama bus (Ⓦ www.peramatour.com), which connects to the daily 13.30 Perama tourist boat departure to the Gili Islands.

BEACHES

The main beach just east of the port is an arc of white sand, which is mainly used to park fishing boats. It's clean and good enough for a quick dip, though, and is right in front of the main clutch of hotels and guesthouses. There are better options just a short walk away, however.

Blue Lagoon

East of the main beach, a signposted path crosses a small headland to end up at this tiny bay with two *warungs* with beach chairs, showers and snorkelling gear. Sunbathing here is nice enough once the hawkers know you're not going to buy anything, but it's the snorkelling and diving that's truly memorable. Even if you just go in knee-deep, you'll see an amazing variety of tropical fish here. The shallow waters here are safe for kids, too.

Pantai Kecil

Walk west past the ferry port over the headland and you'll end up at beautiful 'Small Beach', in a pretty bay with a handful of *warungs*.

THINGS TO SEE & DO

Padangbai is pretty much devoid of sights, but it doesn't really matter because your head's most likely to be submerged under water, gawping at fish. On all three beaches fishermen can take you out on their boats to the better snorkelling spots off Blue Lagoon beach. The diving centres all have their own boats and trustworthy gear for rent.

Geko Dive ⓐ Jalan Silayukti ⓣ (0363) 415 16 Ⓦ www.gekodive.com
ⓛ 08.00–21.00

Pura Silayukti

The largest of the three temples on the eastern headland is dedicated to the priest Empu Kuturan, who is said to have lived here in the 11th century when he introduced the caste system to Bali.

🔺 *The main beach at Padangbai*

Pura Goa Lawah (Bat Cave temple)

This sacred 'directional temple' is situated in front of a massive cave filled with thousands of bats. The cave allegedly runs all the way to Gunung Agung, but it's also believed to be the home of a giant snake god, so it's best to take their word for it. Ceremonies are held here regularly, so you've a good chance of seeing one if you stop by.

ⓐ 4 km (2½ miles) west of Padangbai ⓛ daylight hours ❶ Admission charge

TAKING A BREAK

Restaurants
Puri Rai ££

A pleasantly breezy restaurant overlooking the beach. The chicken sate sizzler plate is memorable, or go for the fresh grilled fish in the evening. ⓐ Jl Silayukti ⓣ (0363) 413 85 ⓛ 08.00–23.00

AFTER DARK

Restaurants & bars
Ozone £

Cheap and cheerful, this café and bar next to the main temple serves local and international food and is a great nightspot to meet other travellers. ⓐ Jl Segara ⓣ (0363) 415 01 ⓛ 09.00–00.00

Nusa Lembongan & Nusa Penida

If you've had quite enough of the unwanted attentions of Bali's many hawkers, jump on a boat to Nusa Lembongan or Nusa Penida, 20 km (12½ miles) off the southeast coast of mainland Bali. These two islands (with one tiny islet in between) offer some of the least touristy escapes in Bali.

Most inhabitants of Nusa Lembongan, the island closest to the mainland, make a decent living off seaweed farming and are too busy to pester tourists with strings of beads or massages. The seaweed industry is quite obvious here – you'll see the square fields in the shallows and will smell it drying upon landing in Jungutbatu village. There are a number of guesthouses and restaurants along the beach here, with some more luxurious digs along the cliff to the west. The best of Lembongan, however, can be found further west and both on and below the waves. A series of pretty bays with white sand (and plenty of drying seaweed) can be found separated by small headlands, with good budget and deluxe hotel resorts overlooking romantic beaches. There's very good surfing off the western tip of the island, and if you venture out with one of the dive centres, you'll see some of Indonesia's best diving spots.

Larger Nusa Penida is a different kettle of fish; hardly visited by tourists and shunned by the Balinese as the home of evil spirits, it has few facilities, but makes up for that by offering stunning scenery of cliffs towering above wild seas, and temples perched on rocky outcrops.

Nusa Lembongan can be seen on a hurried day trip by Scoot Cruise speedboat from Sanur (W www.scootcruise.com), but it's better to stay a night or two. Scoot gets you there in 40 minutes, while cheaper public boats take two hours. Boats to Nusa Penida go from Padangbai or can be chartered from Sanur and Nusa Lembongan.

BEACHES

Nusa Lembongan has better beaches than Nusa Penida, though the main beach at Jungutbatu is crowded with parked boats and the water full of seaweed farms. But it's a short walk or bike ride to better beaches

◔ *Mushroom Bay beach at Nusa Lembongan*

to the west. Note that the water here is cooler than around mainland Bali, and keep an eye on the kids, as the waves can be quite wild.

Coconut & Chelegimbai beaches

Walk west from Jungutbatu on Nusa Lembongan along the clifftop path to reach tiny Coconut and larger Chelegimbai beaches, each with white sand and food and drink stalls.

Dream Beach

Best reached by bike, this quiet bay on Nusa Lembongan's southern coast has a lovely beach.

Mushroom Bay

Nusa Lembongan's best beach is half-an-hour's walk along the path from Jungutbatu or a short bike ride along the inland road. Several hotels and guesthouses fringe the sands and there's great snorkelling just off the beach.

Toyapakeh

Nusa Penida's best beach is at Toyapakeh village, 10 km (6 miles) west of the port town of Sampalan.

THINGS TO SEE & DO

Cycling & motorbiking

Nusa Lembongan's circular road makes for a pleasant cycling trip, and you can cross the pedestrian bridge to tiny Nusa Ceningan, an island sandwiched between the two bigger Nusas. With more stamina, a good map and a full tank of petrol you can tour the steep and winding backroads of Nusa Penida by motorbike to visit the various villages, cliffs and temples.

Drift Divers

One of several diving centres on Nusa Lembongan offering PADI courses and trips. The islands attract serious divers for the clear water and big animals including sharks, mantas and the largest fish on earth, the Ocean Sunfish, or mola mola.

ⓐ Jungutbatu, Nusa Lembongan ⓣ (0366) 244 95
ⓦ www.driftdiverslembongan.com ⓛ 07.00–19.00

Pura Dalem Penataran Ped

This temple near Toyapakeh on Nusa Penida is dedicated to the evil spirit I Macaling, and pilgrims from Bali visit it to appease him, praying he'll stay put on the island.

Sebuluh Cliffs

Near Sebuluh village on the west coast of Nusa Penida, the limestone cliffs rising up from the sea make for some of the most impressive landscapes of Bali.

TAKING A BREAK

Restaurants
Linda's ££

A fine guesthouse restaurant with imaginative and healthy Western food as well as fresh fish. ⓐ Jungutbatu, Nusa Lembongan ⓣ (081) 236 008 67 ⓔ bcwcchoppers@yahoo.com ⓛ 09.00–22.00

Amed

For some really remote R&R, head to Amed – resorts in Bali really don't get much quieter or less touristy than this. It's also a good base for diving and snorkelling around the east coast, especially the famous *Liberty* shipwreck.

'Amed' is actually a string of small fishing villages running for 10 km (6 miles) along the hilly, arid coastline: Amed itself, followed by Congkang, Jemeluk, Bunutan and Lipah (the most developed areas), Lehan, Selang, Banyuning and Aas. There's little public transport here, so your best bets are Perama's tourist shuttle (see page 44) or a private vehicle, taking the main road north from Amlapura and heading east at Culik. There are some nice restaurants, bars and dive centres attached to the hotels, but tourist facilities are extremely sparse – no ATMs or supermarkets, limited phone and internet access – so plan ahead.

BEACHES

The largely undeveloped coast consists of small bays of black- or white-sand beaches, usually lined with fishing boats and sea-salt drying pans. The coastal views are fantastic – especially at **Jemeluk**'s headland – with Gunung Agung behind and neighbouring Lombok across the strait. **Lipah** has the most developed beach in the area.

THINGS TO SEE & DO

Bicycling & trekking

Most hotels have bicycles for hire, helpful for getting around in this very spread-out area. There are some trekking trails up the ridges of **Gunung Seraya** (1,238 m/4,062 ft) – ask at your hotel for a good place to start or if you want to hire a guide.

Diving & snorkelling

The best snorkelling is at Lipah, Selang and Banyuning, where the wreck of a Japanese fishing boat lies near the shore. Most hotels rent out snorkelling gear by the day. The main dive site is at Jemeluk, where a large coral reef offers a wall that's 40 m (131 ft) deep, with lots of tropical marine life. Local operators also offer trips to other sites around the east coast.

Amed Dive Center ⓐ Hotel Uyah Amed, Amed ⓣ (0363) 234 62
ⓦ www.ameddivecenter.com
Eco-Dive Bali ⓐ Jemeluk ⓣ (0363) 234 82 ⓦ www.ecodivebali.com
Euro Dive ⓐ Congkang ⓣ (0363) 234 69 ⓦ www.eurodivebali.com
Wirata Dive School ⓐ Puri Wirata Resort, Bunutan ⓣ (0363) 235 23
ⓦ www.diveamed.com

● *Fishing boats on a beach at Amed*

The 'USS *Liberty*' Wreck

Bali's most popular shipwreck is at **Tulamben**, a 20-minute drive north from Amed. The American military cargo ship USAT *Liberty Glo* (its actual name) was torpedoed by the Japanese in 1942 and beached at Tulamben, where it lay neglected until 1963, when Gunung Agung's massive eruption tumbled it into the sea. It lies in several pieces just 50 m (164 ft) offshore, teeming with coral and fish, but dozens of divers visit daily, so go for early morning or late afternoon to beat the peak hours. Night dives are also spectacular.

TAKING A BREAK

Cafés & bars

Dining options here range from beach *warungs* to hotel restaurants along the main road.

Café Indah £

A beachside *warung* with cheap and classic Indonesian dishes.
ⓐ Lipah ☏ (0363) 234 37 🕒 11.00–21.00

Sunrise £

Another little place on the beach, with fresh fish, seafood and curries.
ⓐ Jemeluk ☏ (0363) 234 77 🕒 08.00–21.30

AFTER DARK

Restaurants & bars
Wawa Wewe II £

Friendly bar and restaurant with live music several nights a week. Standard Western, Indonesian and some Thai dishes with vegetarian and children's options. ⓐ Lipah ☏ (0363) 235 22 🕒 14.00–23.00

Dancing Dragon ££

Well-regarded restaurant offering Asian, European and Balinese dishes prepared with organic ingredients. Vegetarian options galore, and special diets happily catered for. ⓐ Dancing Dragon Cottages, Bunutan ⓣ (0363) 235 21 ⓦ www.dancingdragoncottages.com ⓛ 07.00–22.00

Warung Brith ££

A popular place with authentic Indo-Chinese dishes and *bebek betutu* (see page 92) or *babi guling* (Balinese suckling pig) available with advance order. ⓐ Lipah ⓣ (0363) 235 27 ⓛ 10.00–22.00

🔺 *Bizarre statues in Amed will make you smile!*

Lovina

The antidote to the frantic Kuta scene is surely the chilled-out northern resort known as Lovina, standing for LOVely INdonesiA, a publicity gambit thought up by the last king of the Buleleng regency to attract tourism. It's actually a string of fishing villages 5 km (3 miles) west of Singaraja down the main road Jalan Raya Singaraja, consisting of (from east to west) Pemaron, Tukad Mungga, Anturan, Banyualit, Kalibukbuk and Kaliasem. The restaurants, bars, shops, dive centres and hotels can be found along the main road and the perpendicular streets that run to the beach, with the greatest concentration along Jalans Bina Ria and Mawar in Kalibukbuk, the resort's central area.

If you don't have your own transport, *bemos* run along Jl Raya Singaraja during the day, and *ojek* drivers ply their trade at night. If you decide to hire a motorbike or bicycle here, be aware that this road is quite busy, so always wear a helmet and take care with traffic.

BEACHES

The 8 km (5 miles) of beaches at Lovina are quite different from those down south, consisting mostly of black, pebbly sand with warm, wave-free waters. The offshore reefs keep the ocean calm, a boon for swimmers and snorkellers, but there are no lifeguards here, and be prepared to share the reefs with rows of colourful fishing boats, too.

There's a nice **beachside path** that stretches in either direction from the **dolphin monument** at the end of Kalibukbuk's central Jl Bina Ria, where you'll also find a small market and a number of beachfront cafés. The end of Jl Mawar, the next road eastward, has some more cafés and a popular volleyball court.

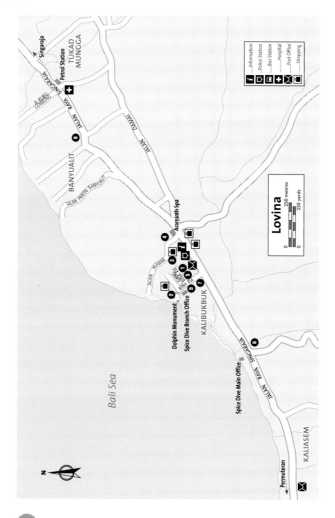

Information
Police Station
Bus Station
Hospital
Post Office
Shopping

Lovina

250 metres
250 yards

Singaraja
TUKAD MUNGGA
Petrol Station

JALAN RAYA SINGARAJA
JL. GURU GEMONG
JALAN DAMAI
BANYUALIT
JALAN PANTAI BANYUALIT
Araminth Spa
JALAN MAWAR
JL. BINA RIA
KALIBUKBUK
Dolphin Monument
Spice Dive Branch Office
Spice Dive Main Office
JALAN RAYA SINGARAJA
KALIASEM
Permuteran

Bali Sea

N

56

THINGS TO SEE & DO

People come to Lovina mostly for its proximity to coral reefs and the slow, relaxing atmosphere. Diving, snorkelling or other watersports, followed by a nice, calming massage, are a typical way to spend a day. For day trip options in the area, see *Excursions From Lovina* (pages 80–84).

Araminth Spa

This wellness spa has different styles of full-body and foot massages, as well as beauty treatments like the classic Javanese *mandi lulur* – a massage followed by a body-mask, exfoliation and final oil massage. If you're really feeling tense, try one of their full-day packages.

ⓐ Jl Mawar, Kalibukbuk ⓣ (0362) 419 01 ⓦ www.lifestylebali.com ⓔ life@lifestylebali.com ⓛ 10.00–19.00 daily

Dolphin watching

You'll see plenty of advertisements for this tourist trap, but if you're expecting a placid little trip with happy dolphins doing trick jumps off your bow, think again. The reality is waking up at dawn to ride in a flotilla of tourist-laden boats frantically chasing after dorsal fins for two early-morning hours. If you're absolutely mad for dolphins you might enjoy it, but otherwise it's probably not worth Rp30,000 and the sacrifice of a morning lie-in.

Spice Dive

Lovina's only five-star PADI dive centre has a branch on Jl Bina Ria, but its main office is on the beach at Kaliasem, west of Kalibukbuk. They offer courses for adults and children, with equipment, lunch and transport included. They also offer packages to dive sites all over Bali, and snorkelling, night diving and watersports like parasailing, wakeboarding and waterskiing. Space Dive's beachside bar and café is also a popular spot for meals or sunset drinks.

ⓐ Kaliasem beach ⓣ (0362) 413 05 ⓦ www.balispicedive.com ⓔ spicedive@balispicedive.com

TAKING A BREAK

Bars & cafés
Bali Apik £ ❶

This laid-back little café features a general and inexpensive tourist menu with Chinese, Indonesian and Western dishes (like Chilli con Carne and pizza), along with a number of vegetarian options. The cold *Bintang* beers are discounted during Happy Hours. ⓐ Gang Bina Ria, off Jl Bina Ria, Kalibukbuk. ❶ (0362) 410 50

Santhi Bar £ ❷

This little beachfront café, right next to Lovina's famous dolphin statue, is perfect for sitting back with a drink or some inexpensive food and watching the waves. ⓐ Lovina Beach, at the end of Jl Bina Ria, Kalibukbuk. ❶ 0852 3720 2147 ❶ 08.00–23.00 daily

⬤ *The dolphin monument in Lovina is proof of its importance here*

AFTER DARK

Restaurants, bars & nightclubs

Almost every hotel here has its own little restaurant. For more options, head to Kalibukbuk, although you'll find the social scene here quiet compared with thumping Kuta.

Barakuda £ ❸

If seafood is your passion, you'll love having the morning's catch – fresh squid, crabs, prawn, lobster and fish – grilled to order and served with any of a dozen different sauces. They also make Balinese classics *babi guling* and *bebek betutu* with a day's advance order.
ⓐ Jl Mawar, Kalibukbuk.

La Madre £ ❹

The cheery owner/chef at this very good little Italian restaurant trained at top restaurants in Seminyak, and her focaccia is baked fresh daily. There are also pasta and meat dishes, and fresh tiramisu if you order the day before. ⓐ Jl Mawar, Kalibukbuk. ❸ (081) 755 43 99

Jasmine Kitchen ££ ❺

This small but airy Thai restaurant off the main road is a real find, with delicious curries and great coffee and desserts. There are tables upstairs and some comfy lounge seating on the ground floor. ⓐ Gang Bina Ria, Kalibukbuk. ❸ (0362) 415 65 ❸ 11.30–22.30 daily

Kwizien ££ ❻

A pleasantly modern European bar and bistro operated by the Belgian owners of Ubud's Café des Artistes, featuring continental European dishes of steaks, poultry and seafood, with a comprehensive wine and beer list. ⓐ Jl Raya Singaraja, Kaliasem ❸ (0362) 420 31 ❸ 11.00–00.00 daily

Poco Evolution Bar ❼

A beach-and-backpackers vibe bar, with occasional live music, screenings of popular films, and a general Indo-Western bar menu. ⓐ Jl Bina Ria, Kalibukbuk ⓣ (0362) 415 35 ⓛ 11.00–01.00

Volcano Club ❽

The only nightclub in the Lovina area, this German-owned place has a bar with garden, pool table, televised sports and a small menu. The dance floor opens at midnight with techno and house beats. It's busiest at weekends and attracts mostly a local crowd with a few tourists. Look for local flyers for more information. ⓐ Jl Raya Singaraja, Anturan ⓛ 21.00–late ❶ Admission charge for dance floor

Zigiz ❾

This cosy little bar on the main street is popular with a mixed clientele of visitors and locals. There's live acoustic music most nights and football on the television. If you're tired of beer, there's a massive cocktail menu to choose from. ⓐ Jl Bina Ria, Kalibukbuk ⓦ www.albe.net/de/zigiz ⓔ zigiz@albe.net ⓛ 18.00–01.00 Sun–Thur, 18.00–02.00 Fri–Sat

Pulau Menjangan & Pemuteran

Pulau Menjangan ('Deer Island') is a small, uninhabited island off Bali's western tip, home to some of Bali's best and most popular diving areas. The clear, shallow, calm waters offer great visibility at seven different sites in the surrounding coral reefs, with spectacular wall dives and multitudes of tropical fish and other marine life like dolphins and turtles. Even for just snorkelling, Pulau Menjangan is a must-see.

The nearby coastal village of Pemuteran, about an hour and a half west of Lovina by car, also has some offshore reefs (including some newly grown as part of an experiment to combat reef loss), but it's generally used more as a base for diving trips. It has a quiet little beach and some lovely accommodation options, so it's also ideal for some 'alone time' far from the crowds.

⬤ *The dock at Pulau Menjangan Island*

BEACHES

Pemuteran's beach is similar to Lovina's, with volcanic black sand, quiet waters, fishing boats and no crowds (or lifeguards).

THINGS TO SEE & DO

Besides diving and snorkelling, your hotel in Pemuteran can also arrange day trips for trekking or birdwatching in **Bali Barat National Park**. Reef Seen Aquatics also offers horse riding and traditional Balinese dance performances.

Reef Seen Aquatics ✆ (0362) 930 01 ⓦ www.reefseen.com
ⓔ dive@reefseen.com

YOS Marine Adventures ✆ (081) 338 779 941 ⓦ www.yosdive.com
ⓔ yosbali@indosat.net.id

Werner Lau Diving Centre ✆ (081) 338 518 512 ⓦ www.wernerlau.com
ⓔ bali@wernerlau.com

TAKING A BREAK

Bars and cafés

All of Pemuteran's hotels, situated along the main road, have their own restaurants, including some specialising in Greek (**Taman Selini ££**
✆ (0362) 947 4688) and Thai cuisine (**Taman Sari ££** ✆ (0362) 932 64).
Or you can try the little *warungs* along the main road for some cheap, delicious Indonesian fare.

◗ *Stone statue of a monkey*

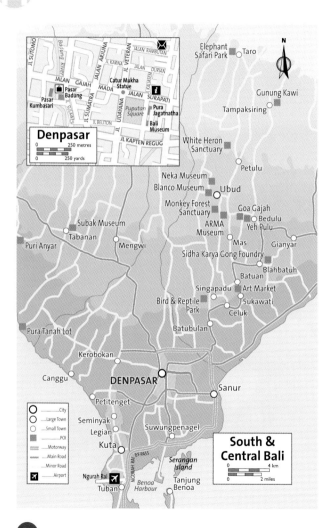

Denpasar

Denpasar is both the provincial capital of Bali and its largest city, with a population of over 400,000. It has only a few attractions of any real interest to tourists but makes for an easy day trip from any of the nearby southern resorts. Hailing a taxi is the most convenient way to go, and not terribly expensive (approximately Rp50,000 from Kuta).

THINGS TO SEE & DO

Most of the things to see here are located near each other in the centre of town and can be covered in a few hours. Start at the four-faced **Catur Mukha Statue**, located at the intersection of Jalans Gajah Mada, Veteran, Surapati and Udayana. It represents the Hindu gods of the cardinal directions and marks the official centre of Denpasar. Directly southeast is **Puputan Square**, a grassy public plaza with a giant bronze statue commemorating the suicidal last stand of the king of Badung and a thousand of his subjects against the Dutch military, which took place here in 1906. On the west side of the square is a state temple, **Pura Jagatnatha**, built in 1953 to honour the supreme Hindu deity, Sanghyang Widi Wasa.

🕐 Daylight hours ❶ Admission by donation; sash and sarong rental. Immediately to its right is the Bali Museum.

Bali Museum

Denpasar's premier tourist attraction is worth a visit for anyone interested in Balinese culture and history. Four separate wings, each built in a different historical and regional architectural style, are situated around a series of picturesque courtyards, and feature exhibits displaying artefacts of Balinese textiles and crafts, religious ceremonies, traditional performing arts, and historical objects, including some grainy photographs of the aftermath of the infamous 1906 *puputan* (ritual suicide) that took place here.

ⓐ Jl Mayor Wisnu ❶ (0361) 222 860 🕐 08.00–15.00 Mon–Thur, 08.00–12.00 Fri, closed Sat & Sun ❶ Admission charge

Turn left from the museum and then right at the next street, following it westward to **Jalan Sulawesi**, a street renowned for its textile and jewellery stores. A right turn will take you north, past shops and street vendors, until you get to **Pasar Badung** on your left. This is Denpasar's largest traditional produce market, and it's worth a wander through the bustle of fruit, vegetable and flower stalls in the courtyard and into the multi-storey building, where more produce, spices and household goods are sold.

Tip: You may find yourselves approached by insistent women who will try to act as your guide and then insist on payment. Tell them 'no' politely and firmly until they go away.

A stone's throw away, just across the sadly unappealing Badung river, is the **Pasar Kumbasari**, a large *pasar seni* (art market). Shoppers will be spoilt for choice with several floors full of inexpensive souvenirs,

⬤ *Historical statues in one of Bali Museum's courtyards*

clothing, sarongs, textiles, baskets, woodcarvings, paintings, masks, jewellery, housewares and other types of arts and crafts. Both markets are just south of Jalan Gajah Mada, a main east–west thoroughfare where you can find a taxi back to your hotel.

TAKING A BREAK

Cafés & bars
As you walk through Denpasar you'll see plenty of local *warungs*, although they cater to a local crowd and you're not likely to find much Western cuisine.

Hawaii Restaurant £
A modest little restaurant with red-chequered plastic tablecloths set inside the Pasar Kumbasari market. It features Chinese and Indonesian dishes and isn't a bad place to stop for a cheap and filling lunch. ➌ Pasar Kumbasari, 1st floor

Restoran Betty £
Only a block away from Jl Sulawesi and the Pasar Badung, this café has a large menu (available in English) full of inexpensive Indonesian dishes, including vegetarian options. ➋ Jl Sumatra 56 🕐 to 21.00 daily

Ubud & around

The Ubud area is the cultural heart of Bali, with the greatest concentration of art museums, dance and musician troupes, and handmade crafts on the island. The beautiful rivers and rice paddies of the surrounding countryside also offer great opportunities for walks, bike rides and recreational activities. As a major tourist area, Ubud also has numerous restaurants, shops and hotels, and is certainly worth a few days' visit if you want something beyond the beach. Just under an hour's drive from Kuta, it's easily accessible by car, *bemo* or tourist shuttle.

THINGS TO SEE & DO

Adventure activities
The countryside is a great place for all sorts of recreational and adventure activities: white-water rafting and kayaking, mountain biking

⬤ *Terraced rice paddies in Ubud's countryside*

or trekking through rice paddies and up mountains, even 4WD tours or elephant safari rides. The two largest companies have a variety of packages for adults and children, including lunch, equipment and free hotel transfers from Ubud and the southern resort areas.

Bali Adventure Tours 🕿 (0361) 721 480 🌐 www.baliadventuretours.com
📧 info@baliadventuretours.com

Bali Sobek 🕿 (0361) 287 059 🌐 www.balisobek.com
📧 sales@balisobek.com

ANIMAL ATTRACTIONS

Monkey Forest Sanctuary

This small forest at the southern end of Ubud is home to several small temples and hundreds of long-tailed grey macaques. They look great in photos, but be careful with your possessions – the wily creatures have learnt to snatch hats and sunglasses and hold them ransom for food. Conveniently, locals sell bags of peanuts for this very purpose.

🅰 Jl Monkey Forest, Ubud 🕿 (0361) 971 304 🕙 08.00–18.00 daily
❗ Admission charge

Tip: These animals are not tame and can get aggressive. Keep your distance and don't try to hand-feed them.

Rimba Reptil (Bali Reptile Park)

Make the kiddies squeal with exhibits of crocodiles, dangerous snakes (including the world's longest python in captivity) and Komodo dragons. Adjacent to the Bali Bird Park.

🅰 Jl Serma Cok Ngurah Gambir, Singapadu 🕿 (0361) 299 344
🕙 09.00–18.00 daily ❗ Admission charge

Taman Burung (Bali Bird Park)

Two hectares of beautifully landscaped gardens feature over 1,000 of our fine feathered friends from all over the world, representing 250 different species – including the endangered Bali Starling. The large restaurant makes a nice place to stop for lunch. Combination tickets are available with the Bali Reptile Park next door.

ⓐ Jl Serma Cok Ngurah Gambir, Singapadu ⓣ (0361) 299 352
ⓦ www.bali-bird-park.com ⓛ 09.00–17.00 daily ❶ Admission charge

ART MUSEUMS
Agung Rai Museum of Art (ARMA)
A large museum displaying local and expatriate artists, with a cultural centre featuring dance performances and workshops in Balinese arts, crafts, history and cookery.
ⓐ Jl Raya Pengosekan, Pengosekan, Ubud ⓣ (0361) 975 742
ⓦ www.armamuseum.com ⓛ 09.00–18.00 daily ❶ Admission charge

The Antonio Blanco Museum
This rather camp museum was once the home of flamboyant Spanish painter and tireless self-promoter Antonio Blanco, who called himself 'the Dali of Bali'. His art demonstrates the endless Western fascination with comely young Balinese women with no tops on.
ⓐ Jl Raya Campuhan, Campuhan, Ubud ⓣ (0361) 975 502
ⓦ www.blancobali.com ⓛ 09.00–17.00 daily ❶ Admission charge

Neka Art Museum
The largest art museum in Bali, featuring over 400 traditional and contemporary works of painting and photography in six different pavilions.
ⓐ Jl Raya Sanggingan, Sanggingan, Ubud ⓣ (0361) 975 074
ⓦ www.museumneka.com ⓛ 09.00–17.00, daily ❶ Admission charge

Crafts villages
Along the roads between Denpasar and Ubud are a number of crafts-producing villages, each known for their own particular speciality. You'll see arts and crafts for sale everywhere on the island (especially in Ubud), but here you can buy directly from the artisans and ask for a tour of the workshops to see them at work: **Batubulan** (stone carvings), **Celuk** (gold and silversmithing), **Sukawati** (local art market and shadow puppets), **Batuan** (painting) and **Mas** (woodcarvings and furniture). Towards Gianyar, the village of **Blahbatuh** has a foundry where metal *gamelan* (traditional musical

instruments) are made and sold along with Balinese dance costumes.

Sidha Karya Gong Foundry Ⓐ Jl Raya Getas–Bururan, Blahbatuh
Ⓣ (0361) 942 798

Dance and music performances

One of the main attractions in Ubud are the nightly performances of traditional Balinese dances and shadow puppet shows, both accompanied by the jangly music of a *gamelan* orchestra. There are several different shows to choose from every night of the week, staged at various venues around Ubud (free transport is provided for the more remote ones). Admission is set at Rp50,000, and the shows last approximately 60–90 minutes. More information and tickets can be found at the Ubud Tourist Information kiosk Ⓐ Jl Raya Ubud Ⓣ (0361) 973 285 or online at Ⓦ www.whatsupbali.com

Tip: If you can see only one show, choose whatever's playing at Puri Saren Agung (Ubud Palace) – the courtyards are a beautiful setting at night.

🔺 *Balinese dances are performed nightly in Ubud*

HISTORICAL SITES

Goa Gajah (Elephant Cave)

This former temple and monastery complex dates back to the 11th century. The cave (used by the monks for meditation) has a fantastically carved entrance of a giant demon's mouth.

ⓐ Jl Raya Goa Gajah, near Bedulu, 4 km (2½ miles) east of Ubud
ⓑ 09.00–17.00 daily ⓘ Admission charge and guide fees

Gunung Kawi

Nine impressively large memorial shrines to an 11th-century Balinese king and his consorts are carved directly into the stone cliffs of a beautiful river valley. A guided walk through the rice paddies takes you to a small waterfall and a tenth shrine, thought to be that of a high minister to the king.

ⓐ Tampaksiring, 12 km (7½ miles) northeast of Ubud ⓑ 08.00–18.00 daily ⓘ Admission charge and guide fees

Yeh Pulu

Just down the road from Goa Gajah are these 14th-century carvings that stretch 25 m (82 ft) across a single wall of rock, depicting scenes from the lives of Hindu gods and heroes and the Balinese people.

ⓐ Tengah, near Bedulu, 5 km (3 miles) east of Ubud ⓑ daylight hours
ⓘ Admission by donation

SHOPPING

The main streets of Ubud – Jalan Raya Ubud, Jalan Monkey Forest and Jalan Hanoman – are chock-a-block with craft shops, art galleries and a large *pasar seni* (art market) selling the handiwork of all the artisanal villages of the surrounding regions. If you don't have time to visit the aforementioned crafts villages, you can still find their products for sale here in Ubud. If there are no visible price tags, be prepared to bargain (see Shopping, page 94).

TAKING A BREAK

Cafés
Gayatri Café £

Family-owned café offering delicious Indian and Indonesian dishes, with plenty of vegetarian options. ⓐ Jl Monkey Forest, Ubud ⓣ (0361) 978 919

Pizza Bagus £

The best pizza in Ubud, just across from the ARMA Museum. Best of all, they deliver. ⓐ Jl Raya Pengosekan, Pengosekan, Ubud ⓣ (0361) 978 520

Naughty Nuri's ££

An Indonesian and Western café favoured by expats, situated across from the Neka Museum. ⓐ Jl Raya Sanggingan, Sanggingan, Ubud ⓣ (0361) 977 547

AFTER DARK

Restaurants & bars

The streets of Ubud are full of terrific restaurants in a variety of cuisines. Local by-laws prohibit much of a nightlife, but there are a few decent bars in town.

Bebek Bengil (Dirty Duck Diner) ££

The speciality of this local favourite is Balinese roast-duck dishes, but they also feature Western dishes and some fantastic desserts. The garden setting is lovely. ⓐ Jl Hanoman, Padangtegal, Ubud ⓣ (0361) 975 489

Bumbu Bali ££

This small water-garden restaurant is known for its delicious fusion menu of Balinese, Indonesian and Indian dishes, with vegetarian options galore. Cookery classes are also available. ⓐ Jl Suweta, Ubud ⓣ (0361) 974 217

Café Lotus ££

Italian and Balinese dishes are served overlooking the beautiful lotus-pond pools of the Pura Saraswati temple, and front-row tables can be reserved for the frequent dance performances held here. Also offers beers from the local microbrewery. ⓐ Jl Raya Ubud, Ubud
ⓣ (0361) 975 660 ⓦ www.lotus-restaurants.com

Jazz Café

Probably the nicest nightspot in town, this stylish garden lounge has cocktails, live jazz music and modern Asian food. ⓐ Jl Sukma, Tebesaya, Ubud ⓣ (0361) 976 594 ⓛ 17.00–00.00 daily

Putra Bar

A popular and casual bar with televised sports and live reggae, jazz and latin music several nights a week. ⓐ Jl Monkey Forest, Ubud ⓣ (0361) 975 570 ⓛ Closes 00.00 daily

Pura Tanah Lot

One of Bali's most sacred temples and probably its most famous, Tanah Lot, is set on a small promontory on the southwestern coast. It's a popular and easy trip from any of the southern resorts and can be arranged through any hotel or tour operator. If using your own transport, head north from Kuta, take the coastal road west at Kerobokan and follow the signs.

THINGS TO SEE & DO

Pura Tanah Lot
Even the touristy souvenir stalls in front of it can't diminish this temple's ruggedly beautiful setting on a rocky islet surrounded by crashing waves. It's one of a string of sea temples (like Pura Luhur Uluwatu, see page 25)

⏶ *Pura Tanah Lot is one of Bali's most sacred temples*

thought to have been built by the Javanese Hindu priest Niratha in the 16th century. The coastal views from the headlands make a striking and photogenic sight, and at low tide you can wade across to the base of the temple and sip holy water from the site's natural underground spring for an extra small donation. (Alas, only worshippers are allowed up to the temple.)

🕐 Daylight hours ❶ Admission charge

VISITING TEMPLES

Temples are extremely sacred places to the Balinese, so it's important to show proper respect whenever you visit one. Please note the following:

- You should wear modest clothing (no bikini tops or bare chests), and you must wear a sarong and a sash around your waist. These can be hired for a small fee at temples if you don't have your own.
- People with fresh wounds and menstruating women are forbidden from entering a temple – the shedding of blood is considered to make one ritually impure.
- Larger temples will charge an admission fee and sometimes a negotiable charge for a tour guide. Smaller temples expect a donation towards upkeep; somewhere between Rp5,000 and Rp10,000 is acceptable.

If you plan to attend a ceremony, please keep these further rules in mind:

- Besides wearing the sarong and sash, try to dress formally: no bare shoulders or T-shirts.
- Do not walk in front of anyone who is praying, or take their photo.
- Do not use a camera flash.
- Do not climb or sit higher than the priest, the offerings or the shrines.

Tip: Sunset at Tanah Lot offers stunning, silhouetted views – and throngs of tourists. Visit earlier in the day to avoid the crowds.

TAKING A BREAK

Cafés & bars
There are numerous food stalls and restaurants situated in and around the temple complex, offering a good range of Indonesian and tourist-orientated fare.

◆ *Tanah Lot temple at sunset looks beautiful*

Royal Water Parks

The last king of the Karangasem regency built several Royal Water Parks in the countryside around his capital (now called Amlapura). Two of them are easily accessible on day trips from the eastern resorts.

THINGS TO SEE & DO

Taman Tirtagangga

Tirtagangga ('Water of the Ganges'), located about 6 km (4 miles) northwest of Amlapura, was built in 1948. It sustained extensive damage during the 1963 eruption of Gunung Agung that devastated much of eastern Bali, but has since been lovingly restored. On a hot day, you can take a refreshing dip in two large swimming pools, but even just a stroll around the four terraced acres makes for a lovely visit. There are landscaped gardens,

⏶ *Statues at Tirtagangga*

placid lily ponds with artfully decorated bridges and floating *bale* pavilions, a striking eleven-tiered water fountain, a large pool with bright orange koi fish, a path of stepping-stones and statues of Hindu gods and heroes, and whimsical animal statues that spout water from the site's underground spring. The upper level offers beautiful ocean and mountain views.
ⓦ www.tirtagangga.com ⓒ 08.00–19.00 daily ⓘ Admission charge; extra fees for swimming pools and guided tours

Taman Ujung

The oldest of the king's parks, Taman Ujung ('At the End') was built in 1921 on the east coast about 5 km (3 miles) south of Amlapura. It was all but destroyed in an earthquake in 1979 but has been renovated in recent years. Its terraced grounds, lined with pools, pavilions and statues, have beautiful ocean views, but there are no pools for swimming and some find it lacks the charm of Tirtagangga.
ⓒ 08.00–17.00 daily ⓘ Admission charge

TAKING A BREAK

Cafés & bars

Both parks have small art markets with food stalls just outside, but Tirtagangga has the advantage of two notable restaurants.

Ryoshi £

Just around the bend from Tirtagangga is this tiny Japanese restaurant, one of an island-wide chain. You'll eat underneath a canopy of tropical flowers, perched on the edge of the valley ridge that offers spectacular views. ⓣ (081) 236 827 91 ⓒ 10.00–22.00 daily

Tirta Ayu Hotel & Restaurant ££

Overlooking the pools from its prime location on the park's upper terrace, this restaurant offers European and Indonesian meals, with vegetarian options, for breakfast, lunch and dinner. ⓣ (0363) 225 03
ⓦ www.hoteltirtagangga.com

Excursions from Lovina

There are a number of sights for easy day trips in the northern region. The area's main city, Singaraja, 5 km (3 miles) east of Lovina, is the second largest after Denpasar, with a population of over 100,000 and two of Bali's best universities. More than anywhere else on the island, Singaraja has had the most foreign influence over the centuries – first as a trading port for ships from Asia, Arabia and Europe, and then as the Dutch colonial capital after their occupation of Bali began in the mid-19th century – and today it has a sizable Chinese and Muslim population. It's not really a tourist town, but if you're in the mood for a wander you could stroll through the colonial buildings at the old harbour, where you'll see the **Yudha Mandala Tama monument** that commemorates the fight for independence from the Dutch and the **Ling Gwan Kiong Chinese temple**.

There's also the inland Bedugul region, home to large botanical gardens and Danau ('Lake') Bratan, only 30 km (18½ miles) south of Singaraja, and hot springs and a Buddhist temple can be found a short drive southwest of Lovina.

THINGS TO SEE & DO

Air Panas Banjar Hot Springs

This popular bathing site offers three decorated stone pools filled with warm, slightly sulphuric water – thought to be especially good for skin ailments – that bubbles up from natural springs on the site. The complex is in a cool and shady spot with some nice gardens, and also has a restaurant, a spa offering massages and an outdoor Jacuzzi (swimsuits required), and changing rooms and lockers.

ⓐ Banjar, 10 km (6 miles) southwest of Lovina ⓑ 08.00–18.00 daily
ⓘ Admission charge

● The pools at Air Panas Banjar Hot Springs

Bali Botanical Gardens

A popular place for picnics when the weather's fine, the Bali Botanical Gardens cover 1.5 sq km (154 hectares) of land in the central region of Bedugul, offering nice views of Danau Bratan. It's got more than 650 kinds of trees, an orchid collection and over 100 different bird species, as well as collections of roses, cacti and bamboo. You can purchase a booklet of six self-guided walks from the ticket office or simply drive your vehicle around the grounds.

ⓐ Candikuning, Bedugul ❶ (0368) 212 73 ❷ 08.00–17.00 daily
❶ Admission and vehicle charges

Brahmavihara Arama

Just a few minutes from the Air Panas Hot Springs is Bali's only Buddhist monastery, located up on a hillside with beautiful ocean views. Like other Buddhist temples in Asia, it features many gilded statues of the Buddha and a Thai-style golden *stupa* (monument). Visitors are asked to dress modestly, speak quietly and remove their shoes as directed. The temple hosts meditation retreats for 10 days each in September and April and is closed to visitors at that time.

ⓐ Banjar, 3 km (2 miles) east of Air Panas ❶ (0362) 929 54
Ⓦ www.brahmaviharaarama.com ❷ Daylight hours ❶ Donation

Pura Meduwe Karang

The land north of the central mountains is slightly more arid, so rice paddies are less common than dry-land crops such as fruit or coffee beans. This important temple is dedicated to the god that protects such crops, and its ornate carvings are considered to be among the finest on the island. Its most famous one is that of a man on a bicycle, thought to be a depiction of a Dutch artist who famously toured Bali on his bike in 1904, sketching scenes of everyday life among the Balinese.

ⓐ Kubutambahan, 11 km (7 miles) east of Singaraja ❷ Daylight hours
❶ Admission by donation; sash and sarong rental

○ *Pura Ulun Danau Bratan is a half-Hindu, half-Buddhist temple*

Pura Ulun Danu Bratan

This beautiful lakeside temple worships the goddess of Danau Bratan, which is one of the main water sources for the rice paddies in central and western Bali. It's also one of the nine most sacred temples on Bali, meant to protect the northwest part of the island from evil spirits. The shrines were originally on small islets only accessible by boat, but since water levels have dropped, they're now on dry land. When the clouds hang low on the lake, however, the multi-tiered *meru* towers almost seem to float above the water. There's also a little market and restaurant if you want to stop for lunch.

ⓐ Danau Bratan, Bedugul ⓒ Daylight hours ⓘ Admission charge

TAKING A BREAK

Cafés & bars

Singaraja has a number of small restaurants and student cafés on its central east–west street, Jalan Jenderal Achmad Yani, and a few more around the corner at its eastern end, on Jalan Gajah Mada. There's also the Pasar Anyar, a food and crafts market just north of Jl Achmad Yani between Jalan Durian and Jalan Diponegoro. Out of the city you'll find food stalls and *warungs* along the main roads.

If visiting the Botanical Gardens or Pura Ulun Danu Bratan in Bedugul, you'll find a number of inexpensive Indonesian restaurants serving the lunchtime trade in Candikuning, a little market town renowned for its local strawberries.

Strawberry Stop £

A roadside café serving just about anything you can make with strawberries – juice, milkshakes, pancakes, ice cream and even wine.

ⓐ 2 km (1¼ mile) north of Candikuning, towards Pancasari
ⓣ (0368) 210 60 ⓒ 08.00–18.00 daily

The Gili Islands

An unlikely combination of revellers, dive fanatics and sun-seekers can be found on **Gili Trawangan**, **Gili Meno** and **Gili Air**, the so-called 'Gili Islands' (*gili* actually means 'island'). These three small islands off the northwest coast of Lombok (the island to the east of Bali) are traffic-free (the taxis are horse carts), have dazzling beaches and superb snorkelling and diving, making them a great short break from Bali. Gili Trawangan is the most developed of the three and has excellent nightlife, with parties most days of the week in high season. Gili Air is quieter and more family-friendly, while Gili Meno is great for getting away from all possible distractions. All three islands have diving centres and there are regular shuttle boats between the islands and to the mainland.

The Gilis can be reached with Perama's tourist boat from Padangbai, departing daily at 13.30, which stops off at all three islands after about a five-hour trip. The 10.00 Perama bus from Kuta connects to this service. The return trip to Bali is by boat to Bangsal on Lombok, a shuttle bus to the nearby resort of Senggigi and the tourist boat from there to Padangbai, arriving around 13.00. It's a few hours quicker and only a little more expensive to fly from Bali to Lombok, take a Blue Bird taxi to Bangsal and hop on a scheduled or charter boat to the islands.

THINGS TO SEE & DO

Relaxing on the beach, sipping fruit juice and cocktails on the open-air *bale* platforms, swimming and diving are the main activities on the Gilis. The diving centres rent out decent snorkelling gear and can book you on the daily glass-bottom boat tour visiting snorkelling sites around all three islands. It's also nice to ride a horse or simply walk around, passing the coconut plantations of the friendly local Muslim population.

Blue Marlin Dive ⓐ Gili Air, Gili Trawangan ⓣ (0370) 634 387
ⓦ www.diveindo.com
Dream Divers ⓐ Gili Trawangan ⓣ (0370) 634 496
ⓦ www.dreamdivers.com ⓛ 08.00–21.30

Horse riding
Stud Horse Riding Adventures ⓐ Gili Trawangan ⓣ (0370) 639 248

Taman Burung (Bird Park)
An aviary park with 400 exotic birds and a Komodo dragon lizard.
ⓐ Gili Meno ⓣ (0370) 642 321 ⓦ www.balipvbgroup.com/gilibirdpark
ⓛ 09.00–17.00

AFTER DARK

Restaurants & bars
All three islands have good and cheap beachside restaurants grilling up
the day's catch, though Trawangan is the island with the most variety of
food. 'Gili T', as it's known among revellers, is famous across Lombok for
its late-night parties in high season; the venue rotates between several
bars, with a party somewhere on most nights of the week.

Tir Na Nog £
A popular Irish restaurant and bar with a huge DVD collection for private
film screenings, pies and sushi on the menu, and a lively atmosphere
even in low season. ⓐ Gili Trawangan ⓣ (0370) 639 463
ⓦ www.tirnanogbar.com ⓛ 09.00–04.00

Vila Ombak ££
The best restaurant on Gili T, with seating in a two-storey wooden
building or on the terrace overlooking the sea. ⓐ Gili Trawangan
ⓣ (0370) 642 336 ⓦ www.hotelombak.com ⓛ 12.00–23.00

ⓞ *Relax by a hotel's swimming pool and palm trees*

Food & drink

Food in Bali ranges from incredibly cheap and modest up through to high gourmet, although Bali is not known for its culinary delights in the same way as other Asian destinations. Ironically, the majority of the 'local' food you'll see on Bali will instead be Indonesian or Chinese in origin, although there are some restaurants that serve classic Balinese cuisine.

WHERE TO EAT

The cheapest (and, some would argue, best) food can always be found at a *warung*, which can range in size from a tiny kiosk to a good-sized restaurant, serving inexpensive Indonesian rice and noodle dishes and a selection of cold drinks or beer. They're great for a quick, cheap meal as they can be found pretty much everywhere, although the seafood *warungs* on Jimbaran's beach are a destination in themselves (see page 26). Larger towns will also often have 'night markets' (*pasar senggol*), where street vendors cook up cheap Indonesian food on the spot; these dishes might be spicier than you're used to, so if you have a delicate stomach, request '*tidak pedas*' ('not spicy').

Most of the mid-range tourist restaurants have larger menus with Indonesian dishes (more expensive than at warungs) and general Western fare: pizza, pasta, salad, sandwiches (plain or toasted 'jaffles'), burgers and chips, chicken, fish and steaks. The Western dishes can vary in quality from 'quite good' to 'simply okay', but the ingredients are always fresh and the food is usually fine as long as you don't expect anything amazing – pizza on Bali is unlikely to be the best you've ever had.

At the top end of the scale, there's quite a bit of high-quality fine dining to be found in the tourist areas, generally around Kuta (especially in Seminyak and Kerobokan), Nusa Dua, Tanjung Benoa and Ubud, often attached to a luxury hotel. While their prices are expensive compared with other restaurants on the island, if you consider them against top restaurants in other parts of the world, they're actually quite reasonable.

The menus can feature anything from specialised European (e.g. French, Greek) or Asian (e.g. Thai, Japanese) cuisines to more modern, East–West fusion cuisine.

Of course, Bali has not been immune to the rise of fast-food chains and convenience stores, either. In the southern resorts and shopping centres you'll see McDonald's, Burger King, KFC and Pizza Hut, as well as Circle K shops and Starbucks.

INDONESIAN DISHES

Most Indonesian cuisine is centred around rice (*nasi*) or noodles (*mie* or *bakmi*). Probably the most iconic dishes are *nasi goreng*, fried rice with bits of vegetables and meat or fish, often accompanied by a fried egg and *krupuk* (prawn crackers), and *mie goreng*, the fried noodle version. There's also *gado-gado* (see 'Vegetarian Options', page 90) and *sate* (sometimes spelled *satay*): bamboo-stick skewers of grilled beef, pork, chicken or fish served with spicy peanut sauce. Streetside food stalls often sell *bakso* (or *soto*) *ayam*, a spicy chicken soup with meatballs and noodles. For a real treat, order *nasi campur*, a large tasting plate consisting of steamed rice surrounded by many small portions of different vegetable, meat and fish dishes (vegetarian versions are sometimes available).

Like much Asian food, food in Bali is quite flavourful and often spicy. Common ingredients are chillies or chilli paste (*sambal*), garlic, lemongrass, kaffir lime, ginger, turmeric, tamarind, coriander, cinnamon and both sweet and sour soya sauces.

BALINESE DISHES

The Balinese generally eat small, modest meals by themselves, whenever they feel hungry – daily meals are not a family affair here. But during religious festivals, all the stops are pulled out and massive feasts are prepared – the origin of many classic Balinese dishes. The two best known are *babi guling*, a suckling pig stuffed and basted with a mixture of herbs and spices and spit-roasted over a low fire, and *bebek betutu*, marinated duck wrapped in banana leaves and roasted on charcoals (sometimes seen as *ayam betutu* and made with chicken) – these dishes usually have to be ordered a day in advance. *Babi guling* is often also served with *lawar*, a salad made with chopped vegetables, coconut, garlic, chilli, minced pork and a little bit of pig's blood, which is sometimes left out for tourists – ask first if you're uncomfortable with the idea. Other common Balinese dishes include *ikan pepes*, fish coated with herbs and spices and steamed in banana leaves, and *sate lilit*, minced fish or seafood with coconut and spices, wrapped around lemongrass stalks like a skewer.

VEGETARIAN OPTIONS

Vegetarians will have little trouble on Bali. Dishes with tofu (soybean curd) and tempeh (fermented soybean cake) are common, and one or both are often included in the delicious *gado-gado*, a dish of blanched vegetables with a mildly spicy peanut sauce (served with prawn crackers, which they'll leave off on request). There are also other vegetable dishes like *cap cai*, a Chinese-style stir-fry, and vegetarian versions of dishes like *nasi campur* are often available. Cooks will generally be happy to make something vegetarian upon request.

ALCOHOLIC DRINKS

The most popular local beer here is *Bintang*, a cheap and light lager that's quite refreshing on a hot day. You'll also see *Anker* and the (rather unappealing) *Bali Hai*. The best local beers come from the Storm microbrewery, which produces flavoursome ales and stouts (Ⓦ www.stormbrewing.net). Many well-known Asian and Western beers are also imported.

Grapes from northern Bali are used to make the local wine brand Hatten; their rosé is one of the best and most popular of these. Wine of the Gods is another local brand but uses imported Australian grapes. You'll find much better Australian and European wines at many restaurants, but naturally they'll be more expensive.

Traditional Balinese spirits include *tuak*, a sweetish palm wine (approximately 5% proof), and *brem*, a slightly stronger, somewhat pungent fermented rice wine, but the best is *arak*, a clear, distilled palm spirit that packs a stronger punch (around 80% proof) and is often served with orange or lemon juice and honey – a much cheaper alternative to drinks with name-brand spirits if you're really in a drinking mood.

RESTAURANT ETIQUETTE

Service at most *warungs* and many restaurants in Bali is cheerful as a rule, but may seem much slower than at home; keep in mind that the concept of time here is more elastic, and anyway, you're on holiday, so where do you have to rush off to? If you're with a group at a small *warung*, be aware that your dishes will probably not arrive at the same time – the cook often has only one burner to use for preparing everything, so just eat whenever you're served. For information on tipping, see During your stay (page 122).

COOKERY CLASSES

Food lovers can learn how to prepare Balinese cuisine at the half-day classes (usually incorporating a market visit) offered in many tourist areas, especially down south and in Ubud – look for advertisements or enquire at your hotel. A particularly good one is given by Heinz von Holzen, a top Swiss chef and international expert on Balinese food, at his Bumbu Bali restaurant in Tanjung Benoa. For more information, see Ⓦ www.balifoods.com or Ⓦ www.indo-chef.com

Menu decoder

Restaurants in tourist resorts will always have English-language menus, but some smaller *warungs* may have menus partly or mostly in Indonesian.

INGREDIENTS
Ayam Chicken
Babi Pork
Bebek Duck
Daging Meat
Ikan Fish
Kepiting Crab
Mie Noodles
Nasi Rice
Sapi Beef
Sayur Vegetables
Tahu Tofu
Telur Egg
Tempeh A patty of fermented soybeans, with a slightly nutty taste
Udang Prawn

EXTRAS
Garam Salt
Gula Sugar
Kare Curry
Kecap asam Sour soy sauce
Krupuk Prawn crackers
Lada Pepper
Sambal A spicy chilli paste or sauce, made in a variety of flavours

DISHES
Ayam bakar Grilled chicken
Ayam pelalah Shredded chicken served with chillis and lime

Bakso/Soto ayam Spicy chicken soup with noodles and meatballs
Bebek betutu Spicy marinated duck steamed in wrapped banana leaves – usually requires advance order
Cap cai Chinese-style sautéed vegetables
Ikan pepes Fish basted with spices and steamed in banana leaves
Lumpia Spring rolls
Mie goreng Fried noodles with vegetables and sometimes meat or seafood
Nasi campur A large tasting plate consisting of steamed rice surrounded by numerous small portions of different meats, vegetables and sambals, but also available as a vegetarian dish
Nasi goreng Indonesia's most iconic dish – fried rice with bits of vegetables and sometimes meat or seafood, often served with a fried egg on top and eaten at breakfast
Opor ayam Chicken with coconut curry
Pisang goreng Fried banana fritters

Rendang Beef with coconut curry

Rijsttafel A Dutch/Indonesian multi-course meal, consisting of numerous different meat, fish, seafood and vegetables dishes served with rice

Sate or **satay** Skewers of grilled meat or fish, served with spicy peanut or other kinds of sauce

BEVERAGES

Air minum Drinking water

Arak A clear spirit distilled from palm sap

Bir Beer

Brem Rice brandy

Es Ice

Jus jeruk manis Orange juice

Jus jeruk nipis Lemon juice and water (available sweetened or plain)

Kopi Coffee

Kopi susu Coffee with milk

Teh Tea

Teh limon Tea with lemon

Tuak Palm wine

TROPICAL FRUITS

Blimbing Starfruit

Jambu Guava

Jeruk manis Orange – don't be put off by the bright green rind; they're actually ripe

Jeruk nipis Lemon

Kelapa Coconut

Manggis Mangosteen – has a thick, deep-red skin and white fleshy fruit inside

Nanas Pineapple

Nangka Jackfruit – a gigantic, knobby rind filled with sweet, fleshy seed-sheath fruits

Pisang Banana – a shorter version of those sold in Western countries

Rambutan ('Hairy fruit') – a bright red fruit with soft, wiry 'hairs' coming off it. Open it with your fingers to get at the sweet, translucent fruit underneath

General words and phrases:

Daftar makanan Menu

Garpu Fork

Pisau Knife

Satu lagi One more

Saya seorang vegetarian I'm a vegetarian

Saya tidak suka makan... I don't eat...

(Tidak) pedas (Not) spicy

Tolong nota The bill, please

Tolong tanpa es Without ice, please

Tolong tanpa gula Without sugar, please

Shopping

Shopping is a major tourist attraction on Bali, where visitors can find both local handmade crafts and imported international brands at lower prices than back home. The big tourist areas of Kuta and Nusa Dua have ultra-modern shopping centres – a good place for Western brands and English-language bookstores – but you'll also see plenty of small shops, especially around Kuta, and nearly every tourist town will have at least one *pasar seni* (art market) with stalls selling arts, handicrafts, clothing and souvenirs. You can also expect to be approached regularly in most tourist areas by street hawkers (see Kuta and Around, page 19). They and some of the smaller shops aren't always likely to take credit cards, so have some cash handy and be prepared to bargain (see page 96).

⬤ *Typical baskets and rugs made in the craft villages*

ART & HANDICRAFTS

The craft villages between Denpasar and Ubud (see page 70) produce most of the traditional handicrafts in Bali: silver and gold jewellery and accessories, wood and stone carvings and sculptures, Javanese-style shadow puppets, masks, pottery, baskets, rugs, home décor and musical instruments. You'll find their work for sale in Ubud and art markets all over the island, although you can also go straight to the source for custom-designed work.

Ubud and the surrounding area is also known for many vibrant styles of both traditional and modern Balinese painting. Often named after the areas best known for them, such as Kamasan, Ubud, Batuan and Pengosekan, the subjects ranging from epic stories of Hindu gods to portraits of ordinary life or colourful animals and plants. Enquire about buying paintings without the frames for easier transport home.

CLOTHING & TEXTILES

The streets of Kuta, Legian and Seminyak – and especially Kuta Square – are lined with clothing stores with Western-style fashions for adults and kids. Expect light resort-wear, batik clothing and tropical prints. You'll see local stores like Body & Soul, Paul Ropp, By the Sea, Kuta Kidz, Blush Deluxe and Uluwatu, which specialises in handmade lace clothing, nightwear and linens.

In the huge, modern shopping centres scattered around the southern resort areas (see page 97), you'll find discounted outlets for international high-fashion brands (Polo, Prada, Armani, Versace, etc.), sportswear (Nike, Quiksilver, Ripcurl, etc.) and perfumes and cosmetics (Revlon, Clinique, Estee Lauder, etc.), not to mention food courts with KFC, Pizza Hut and Starbucks – you may feel as though you never left home.

If you want more local Balinese and Indonesian styles, you won't have trouble finding plenty of shops and art-market stalls selling batik clothing and sarongs, and especially the traditional *ikat* weaving style, in which warp or weft threads are dyed before weaving, resulting in intricate patterns that can take skilled weavers many months to produce. Even more precious is cloth in the double-*ikat* style (in which both threads are dyed), made only in the traditional Balinese village of Tenganan (see page 41). Gold and silver threads are also worked in to make the rich brocade *songket*, often used for dancer's costumes. Try Jalan Sulawesi in downtown Denpasar (see page 66) for a large concentration of Indonesian clothing and textile stores, or for *ikat* clothing and home décor try **Nogo Ikat Centre** (ⓐ Jl Danau Tamblingan 104, Sanur ❶ (0361) 288 765 ⓦ www.nogobali.com ❷ 09.00–21.00 daily) or **Threads of Life**, which also offers workshops in traditional textiles and day trips to local workshops (ⓐ Jl Kajeng 24, Ubud ❶ (0361) 972 187 ⓦ www.threadsoflife.com).

FURNITURE

Although you can't find much in the way of real antiques – Indonesian law prohibits the export of items older than fifty years – you can purchase reproductions and new pieces of handsome Indonesian teak

HOW TO BARGAIN

If you're buying from street vendors, art markets or shops where the merchandise has no price tags, you'll be expected to bargain for your purchases. It's a good idea to do a bit of window-shopping in the area first to compare prices and quality. When you're ready to buy, ask a vendor for a price, and then give a counter-offer that's about one-third of that. You'll then negotiate back and forth until you reach a price that's between one-half and two-thirds of the original offer. If the seller's final offer is still more than you want to pay, just thank them and walk away: you'll usually be called back within seconds for your last offer. Even if this doesn't happen, the same goods will generally be available at another shop nearby.

and bamboo furniture. Make sure to inspect pieces closely for rot or termites, and ask whether the wood has been properly dried, otherwise the different humidity of your home climate could cause cracking. There are a number of furniture stores along the main road in Seminyak and Kerobokan, at the northern end of the Kuta area, as well as on Ngurah Rai Bypass road between Kuta and Sanur. Some stores can arrange shipping home, or else try one of the international courier services who have offices in Bali, generally located in Denpasar, Kuta and/or Ubud (see box below).

DEPARTMENT STORES

Matahari A large department store chain with a supermarket and fixed-price general merchandise such as books, clothes, shoes, gifts, electronics, etc. – a good place to stock up on anything you forgot to pack. Four locations around Kuta and Denpasar. Ⓦ www.matahari.co.id
ⓐ Kuta Square, Kuta ⓣ (0361) 757 588 Ⓛ 10.00–22.00 daily
ⓐ Jl Legian, Legian, Kuta ⓣ (0361) 754 195
ⓐ Bali Galleria, Jl Bypass Ngurah Rai, Simpang Siur, Kuta
ⓣ (0361) 755 277
ⓐ Jl Dewi Sartika, Denpasar ⓣ (0361) 237 365

SHOPPING CENTRES

Bali Collection
ⓐ Jl Pratama, Nusa Dua ⓣ (0361) 771 662 Ⓦ www.bali-collection.com

INTERNATIONAL SHIPPING COMPANIES
DHL ⓣ (0361) 762 138 Ⓦ www.dhl.co.id
FedEx ⓣ (0361) 701 727 Ⓦ www.fedex.com/id
TNT ⓣ (0361) 703 519 Ⓦ www.tnt.com
UPS ⓣ (0361) 756 148 Ⓦ www.ups.com

Discovery Shopping Mall
@ Jl Kartika Plaza, Tuban, Kuta ☎ (0361) 755 522
ⓦ www.discoveryshoppingmall.com 🕐 10.00–23.00
Mal Bali Galleria
@ Jl Bypass Ngurah Rai, Simpang Siur roundabout, Kuta ☎ (0361) 237 364
🕐 09.00–18.00 or later (varies by store)

SUPERMARKETS

Bintang
@ Jl Raya Seminyak 17, Seminyak, Kuta ☎ (0361) 730 552 🕐 08.00–23.00
@ Jl Raya Campuhan 45, Campuhan, Ubud ☎ (0361) 972 972
🕐 08.00–22.00

Children

Children are universally welcomed on Bali, and there are plenty of activities to entertain them beyond a day at the beach. Most large hotels also offer babysitting or children's clubs with daycare and arts and crafts, and some have wading pools or other outdoor activities tailored for kids. Many restaurant staff will even be happy to watch your kids for you while you enjoy your meal. Try ⓦ www.baliforfamilies.com and ⓦ www.balifamilyholidays.com for more information.

ADVENTURE ACTIVITIES

Bali Adventure Tours and **Bali Sobek** have river rafting, biking and trekking around the Ubud area (see pages 68–9), suitable for families with children at least 7 years old.
Bali Treetop Adventure Park, located in the Bali Botanical Gardens (see page 82), has rope bridges and swings, flying-fox lines and climbing circuits for all ages, with full safety harnesses. ⓐ Candikuning, Bedugul ⓣ (081) 338 306 898 ⓦ www.balitreetop.com ⓛ 08.30–18.00 daily

Animal parks
There are a number of attractions near Ubud: the **Bali Bird & Reptile Parks** and the **Monkey Forest Sanctuary** (see page 69), as well as the **Bali Zoo Park** (ⓐ Jl Raya Singapadu, Singapadu ⓣ (0361) 294 356 ⓛ 09.00–18.00 daily ⓘ Admission charge), and the **Elephant Safari Park**, which is run by Bali Adventure Tours and included in many of their packages (ⓐ Taro, 18 km (11 miles) north of Ubud ⓣ (0361) 721 480 ⓛ 09.00–17.00 daily ⓘ Admission charge).
Pura Luhur Uluwatu (see page 25) is home to troupes of wild macaques, but as with those in the Monkey Forest Sanctuary, they're not tame animals and small children might get frightened.

Horse riding
Umalas Stables, Kerobokan, Kuta area (see page 18).

Paintball

Paintball Bali has a large site near Nusa Dua with the latest equipment and safety-wear imported from the US. Players must be at least 12 years old. ⓐ Jl Karang Putih 1, Jabapura, Bukit Badung ⓣ (0361) 770 300 ⓦ www.paintballbali.com ⓔ info@paintballbali.com ⓛ 09.00–21.00 daily

Water parks

Waterbom Bali water park, Tuban, Kuta area (see page 21).

Watersports

Many diving and surf schools in the Kuta area (see page 21) have children's courses. Tanjung Benoa (see page 37) and Sanur (see page 29) have watersports like parasailing, waterskiing and banana-boat rides.

TIPS AND ADVICE

- Remember to use protective clothes, sunscreen and bottled water to protect your children from the strong sun and heat.
- Streets can be broken or bumpy and kerbs are high. Rubber-wheeled strollers or shoulder harnesses are best for carrying little ones.
- Disposable nappies can be bought in supermarkets, but they can be expensive. It's often best to bring your own or use cloth nappies.
- Large families might find it easier to hire a private driver with a minivan than to use public transport or taxis.
- Don't get temporary tattoos in Bali, as the dyes used can be unsafe.

Sports & activities

There are plenty of sporting and recreational activities to be found everywhere on Bali: in the ocean and rivers, the fields and the mountains, or even just the massage room of a comfortable spa. Specific listings are given within individual sections as noted.

ADVENTURE ACTIVITIES

Two large companies, **Bali Adventure Tours** and **Bali Sobek**, offer white-water rafting and kayaking, mountain bike trips and jungle or rice-paddy treks out in the countryside around Ubud (see page 68). If you fancy getting your feet off the ground, Bali Adventure Tours also offers paragliding, parasailing can be found in Tanjung Benoa (see page 37), and there's also bungy jumping, kite surfing and skydiving in the southern resorts.

AJ Hackett Bungy Jump ⓐ Jl Pantai Double Six, Legian, Kuta
ⓣ (0361) 731 144 ⓦ www.aj-hackett.com
Bali Kite Surf ⓐ Nusa Dua ⓣ (081) 139 39 19 ⓦ www.balikitesurf.com
Bali Paragliders Club ⓐ Jl Bypass Ngurah Rai 12A, Kuta ⓣ (0361) 704 769
ⓦ www.balipargliders.com
Skydive Bali ⓣ (0361) 764 210

DIVING & SNORKELLING

Bali is surrounded by tropical coral reefs, which make for some truly incredible underwater experiences. The top site is generally considered the tiny island of Pulau Menjangan (see page 61), but other great spots include Candidasa (see page 39), Padangbai (see page 44), Amed (see page 51) and the *Liberty* wreck at Tulamben (see page 53).

GOLF

There are two world-class 18-hole courses near the southern resorts, one in Nusa Dua (see page 35), and the Greg Norman-designed **Le Meridien Nirwana**, which overlooks the ocean near Pura Tanah Lot (@ Tabanan ☎ (0361) 815 960 ⓦ www.nirwanabaligolf.com).

HORSE RIDING

There are some lovely beach rides from stables north of Kuta (see page 18) and in Pemuteran (see page 61).

MOUNTAIN CLIMBS

The central volcanoes of east Bali are popular for sunrise climbs, but are challenging and should be undertaken only by the fit and healthy.

PAINTBALL

Listed under Children (see page 100).

SPAS

Bali takes its 'paradise' reputation seriously, and many hotels offer full-service spas for massage and beauty treatments, usually also open to the public. There's a nice little spa in Lovina (see page 57), in Ubud the **Hotel Tjampuhan** has one in a picturesque riverside spot (@ Jl Raya Campuhan ☎ (0361) 975 368 ⓦ www.indo.com/hotels/tjampuhan) and in Seminyak the grand **Prana Spa & Villas** is decorated to look like an Indian palace (@ Jl Kunti 118X ☎ (0361) 730 840 ⓦ www.thevillas.net). For a real treat, try the *mandi lulur*, a full-body massage and exfoliation with fragrant herbs and spices.

SURFING

Bali is renowned for its fantastic surfing breaks, all located down south. Kuta (see page 14) is the granddaddy of them all – and there are plenty of surf schools there if you want to learn – but more advanced and discerning tastes will appreciate the beaches at the southwestern end of the Bukit peninsula (see page 26) or those on Nusa Lembongan (see page 47).

WATERSPORTS

The calm waters at Sanur (see page 29) and Tanjung Benoa (see page 35) are fantastic for watersports such as jetskiing, waterskiing and boat rides. The top dive centre in Lovina (see page 55) also offers some. There's also a water park in the Kuta area (see page 21).

⬥ *Surfing is popular with locals and tourists alike*

Festivals & events

Religious festivals take place regularly on Bali, calculated by a lunar-based calendar of 210 days called *pawukon*. Every temple has a three-day *odalan* (anniversary ceremony), and there are numerous other Hindu holidays throughout the year, so if you want to observe a ceremony somewhere near you, enquire with your hotel or a tourist office for a schedule of dates. Non-religious cultural and sporting events have also started up in recent years thanks to Bali's popularity as a holiday destination.

RELIGIOUS EVENTS

Galungan & Kuningan

Galungan is a ten-day festival held in the 11th week of the *pawukon* calendar. The Balinese gather in their villages to feast and celebrate with

⬤ *One of Bali's frequent temple ceremonies*

family and friends and welcome the return of the souls of their ancestors. On the final day, Kunigan, everyone says goodbye to their family's spirits, who return to heaven to live with the gods.

Nyepi

Also known as 'the day of silence', Nyepi is the Balinese New Year, held in March or April. The night before, evil spirits are chased away from the island by raucously noisy parades featuring papier-mâché monsters called *ogoh-ogoh*, which are burnt in effigy. On Nyepi itself, everyone on Bali stays quietly inside their homes for the entire day so the evil spirits will think the island is empty and thus not worth bothering with. All flights are cancelled, all businesses, restaurants and shops are closed, and tourists are expected to remain within the confines of their hotels for the day.

CULTURAL EVENTS

Bali Arts Festival

A huge, one-month celebration of performing arts that starts in June, with numerous performances staged daily in Denpasar, along with food and handicrafts stalls and historical exhibitions.

ⓦ www.baliartsfestival.com

Bali Kite Festival

Held in June or July near Sanur, this event attracts hundreds of teams with huge kites built in the shapes of animals, demons, machines and anything else they can get airborne.

Chinese New Year

The estimated 150,000 Chinese–Balinese are descendants of Chinese traders who migrated here as early as the 7th century. Locals and Chinese visitors celebrate the New Year (held in January or February) with parades, fireworks and dragon dances.

Kuta Karnival

A nine-day 'celebration of life' offering sporting competitions, kite flying, parades, food stalls, live music and nightly dances. Check the website for current dates. Ⓦ www.kutakarnival.com

Ubud Writers and Readers Festival

Held each September, it features international authors and a week of presentations, workshops and children's events.
Ⓦ www.ubudwritersfestival.com

SPORTING EVENTS

Wismilak International

An official WTA tennis tournament, the biggest in Southeast Asia, with internationally high-ranked players. Held every September in Nusa Dua.
Ⓦ www.wismilakinternational.com

Indonesian Surfing Championships

Bali's world-renowned surfing beaches host a number of events on the Indonesian Pro Surfing Tour, with various dates and locations.
Ⓦ www.light-indo.com/ISC

▶ *Road signs at Amed*

Preparing to go

GETTING THERE

By air

Many major carriers offer direct flights to Bali/Denpasar (DPS), with at least one stop and code-sharing with a partner airline. (At time of writing, only Australia's Jetstar Ⓦ www.jetstar.com.au offers a non-stop service to Bali, from Melbourne and Sydney.) It's easiest to start with global travel websites such as **Expedia** (Ⓦ www.expedia.co.uk), **Travelocity** (Ⓦ www.travelocity.co.uk) or **STA Travel** (Ⓦ www.statravel.co.uk), although you can also try some of the airlines directly.

Many people are aware that air travel emits CO_2, which contributes to climate change. You may be interested in the possibility of lessening the environmental impact of your flight through the charity Climate Care, which offsets your CO_2 by funding environmental projects around the world. Visit Ⓦ www.climatecare.org

British Airways ☎ 0870 850 9850 Ⓦ www.britishairways.com
Cathay Pacific ☎ 020 8834 8888 Ⓦ www.cathaypacific.com
KLM ☎ 0870 507 4074 Ⓦ www.klm.com
Malaysia Airlines ☎ 0870 607 9090 Ⓦ www.malaysiaairlines.com

PACKAGE TOUR OPERATORS

There are many operators offering package and custom tours to Bali for singles, couples or families:

The Adventure Company ☎ 0845 4505316
Ⓦ www.adventurecompany.co.uk
Audley Travel ☎ 01993 838 100 Ⓦ www.audleytravel.com
Hayes and Jarvis ☎ 0870 366 1636 Ⓦ www.hayesandjarvis.co.uk
Kuoni Travel ☎ 01306 747 002 Ⓦ www.kuoni.co.uk
Magic of the Orient ☎ 0117 311 6050 Ⓦ www.magicoftheorient.com
Thomas Cook ☎ 0870 443 4447 Ⓦ www.thomascook.com

Qantas ☎ 0845 774 7767 🌐 www.qantas.com
Singapore Airlines ☎ 0870 608 8886 🌐 www.singaporeair.com
Thai Airways ☎ 0870 606 0911 🌐 www.thaiair.com
Indonesia's national airline is **Garuda** (☎ 020 7467 8600 🌐 www.garuda-indonesia.com), but be aware that it has had some accidents and safety issues in recent years.

TOURISM AUTHORITY
Bali's district capitals have government-run tourist offices, but help is usually limited to brochures or schedules of religious ceremonies.
Bali Tourism Board 🏠 Jl Raya Puputan 41, Denpasar ☎ (0361) 235 600
🌐 www.bali-tourism-board.com 📧 info@bali-tourism-board.com
Good information and listings can also be found at sites like these:
🌐 www.baliblog.com
🌐 www.baliplus.com
🌐 www.bali-paradise.com
🌐 www.whatsupbali.com

BEFORE YOU LEAVE
Ensure your vaccinations (typhoid, hepatitis A/B, tuberculosis, etc.) are up to date before visiting Southeast Asia. Talk to your doctor or check

TRAVEL INSURANCE
Bali has no reciprocal medical schemes, so it's important to purchase travel insurance beforehand, as serious accidents or illnesses there may require evacuation to Singapore or your home country for treatment. Check the policy carefully regarding medical coverage, loss of baggage, repatriation, etc., and whether recreational activities like scuba diving, white-water rafting or bungy jumping need extra coverage. Keep all medical receipts for claim purposes; if your possessions are stolen, you'll also need to file a police report.

⬤ *Colourful woodcarving of Garuda – a bird-like creature in Hindu and Buddhist mythology*

www.mdtravelhealth.com or your government's travel advisory
website for the latest information.

Bring enough of your prescription medicine to last the trip –
pharmacies here stock a wide range but dosages may be different. Bring
a sun hat, sunblock and a basic first-aid kit for cuts, or you can purchase
them in resort areas.

ENTRY FORMALITIES

Citizens of the UK, Ireland, EU countries, USA, Canada, Australia, New
Zealand, and South Africa must purchase a tourist visa on arrival at the
airport: US$10 for 7 days or US$25 for 30 days (four-month visas will be
offered in future), payable by cash or credit card. The visa cannot be
extended or converted; overstays are charged at US$20 per day. Passports
must be valid for six months from entry date; proof of intended
departure is required (though seldom checked). Don't lose your
disembarkation card: it's required on departure.

CUSTOMS ALLOWANCES

You're allowed the following items: 200 cigarettes, 50 cigars or 100
grams of tobacco, one litre of alcohol, perfume for personal use, and up
to 10 million Rupiah. Strictly prohibited are narcotic and psychotropic
drugs, weapons and ammunition, pornographic materials and printed
matter in Chinese. Pre-recorded videotapes and discs may be censored
and animals, fish and plants are subject to quarantine.

Departure tax

An airport departure tax is payable in cash only: Rp100,000 (international
flights) and Rp30,000 (domestic) from Bali, and Rp30,000 from Lombok.

MONEY

Indonesia uses the Rupiah (Rp). The most commonly used notes are
100,000, 50,000, 20,000, 10,000, 5,000 and 1,000, with coins in 1,000,
500, 200 and 100. Break into larger notes in busy areas and hang on to
smaller change if you're planning to visit more outlying areas (especially
the Gili Islands) or use public transport.

International ATMs are readily found at the airport, in large towns and most tourist resorts (except for Candidasa and Amed, at time of writing). Notes are dispensed as Rp100,000 or 50,000. ATMs are uncommon or unavailable in small towns and more remote areas, so plan ahead. Avoid money-changers if possible. Mid-range and high-end hotels, shops and restaurants in tourist centres accept major credit cards (usually Visa/Mastercard) but charge a 3–5 per cent transaction fee.

CLIMATE

Bali has warm and constant temperatures year-round, with a daytime average of 27°C (80°F) on the coasts and 22°C (72°F) in higher inland regions. Night-time temperatures dip only a few degrees and are still quite comfortable, though it gets cooler inland and some might want a light jacket in these areas. The equatorial sun can get quite hot, so beware sunburn.

The two seasons are dry (April to October) and rainy (November to March); December and January are the wettest. Humidity is usually around 75 per cent in the dry season and gets up to a sweaty 90 per cent in rainy months (most hotels offer air conditioning).

Don't be put off by the idea of a rainy-season visit: tropical rains can be unpredictable and heavy, but generally fall for only an hour or so before the hot, sunny weather returns – and in this low tourist season, resorts are less crowded and many goods and services are discounted or can be negotiated down further.

BAGGAGE ALLOWANCE

Check with airlines in advance, as regulations can change frequently. Most generally allow up to 20 kg (44 lb) of luggage per person for an economy ticket, but bulky items such as surfboards may incur extra fees.

During your stay

AIRPORTS

Bali has one airport to handle all domestic and international flights:
Ngurah Rai International Airport (DPS) 🅐 Tuban, Denpasar
(3 km/2 miles south of Kuta) 🕿 (0361) 751 011
🌐 www.angkasapura1.co.id/eng/location/bali.htm
Hotel transfers are often available by advance request – enquire when
booking. Fixed-price taxis are available to popular destinations: tickets
are purchased at the signed counter in the arrivals hall and then given
to the driver. To save some money on trips to the Kuta area, turn right
outside the terminal, walk approximately 500 m (⅓ mile) and exit
through the front gates to catch a metered 'Blue Bird' taxi waiting

TELEPHONE CODES

The country code for **Indonesia** is **62**. To call Bali from abroad, dial
your local international access code (UK, Ireland, South Africa, New
Zealand: 00; US, Canada: 011; Australia: 0011) or use a + if on a
mobile phone, then 62 and the area code (omitting the first 0) and
local number.

Telephoning abroad

To call from Bali, dial 001 (or + if on a mobile) followed by country
code, area code (omitting first 0 if required) and local number.
England 44 **US & Canada** 1 **Australia** 61 **Ireland** 353 **New Zealand** 64
South Africa 27

Helpful numbers

International Operator 🕿 101
International Directory Assistance 🕿 102
Domestic Operator 🕿 100
Local Directory Assistance 🕿 108

outside. Beware of transport touts who may insist on taking you to 'a friend's hotel'.

Flying between Bali and Lombok (if visiting the Gili Islands) will take you through Lombok's sole airport: **Selaparang Airport (AMI)** ❸ Located in Rembiga (2 km/1 mile north of Mataram), Lombok.

POSTAL SERVICES

Every town has a *kantor pos* (general post office), which generally follows bank hours (see **Opening Hours**). You can also buy stamps and postcards and post letters at various independent postal agents who will have shops in towns and tourist areas. Post boxes (*bis surat*) are small, square and orange but infrequently found. Stamp prices vary according to weight and destination; expect to pay between Rp6,000 and Rp12,000 for international postcards and allow two weeks' delivery time. International delivery services such as FedEx, DHL, UPS and TNT have offices in major tourist centres such as Kuta and Ubud if you want to ship any valuable parcels overseas.

INTERNET ACCESS

Many major hotels now feature in-room internet for either wireless or ethernet connections, or at least have internet terminals for guest use on-site. Internet cafés can be found in all tourist resorts, although the speed and price can vary by location. In the Kuta area, you can expect to pay approximately Rp200 per minute for decent broadband speeds, while cafés in Candidasa, for example, offer only dial-up modem speeds at three times the price (at time of writing).

CUSTOMS

The Balinese are friendly, hospitable and polite people, and put great store on good manners, especially in public. Shouting or swearing over minor issues with goods or services will be seen as very rude.

Never touch anyone's head (even a child's), as the Hindu Balinese believe it to be the holiest part of the body. Always give and receive only with the right hand; the left is considered unclean. Avoid pointing

at someone or something with an index finger; use the right
thumb instead.

Most Balinese or other Indonesians working in hospitality or tourist
services will have a good command of English. As Indonesian is a fairly
simple language to pick up, it's worth learning at least a few phrases –
you will find your attempts to speak it met warmly by locals.

DRESS CODES

Within tourist areas, short and casual clothes with bare arms and legs
are fine, but topless sunbathing is not generally recommended outside
Nusa Dua (especially in the Gili Islands, where the locals are Muslim).
Some high-end restaurants and nightclubs will request 'smart casual'
dress at night. In small villages and rural areas, clothing that is too short
may be seen as immodest, so it's good to have a shirt to cover your
shoulders and a sarong to wrap around your waist.

Temples are sacred ground, so dress modestly if visiting one. Wearing
a sarong and a sash is required, but many temples have these available
for hire if you do not have your own.

ELECTRICITY

Bali uses 220 V electricity with two-pin (*schuko*) plugs. Plug adaptors are
sometimes available at high-end hotels or may be purchased from shops
in large tourist areas. Visitors from the US and Canada will also need a
voltage converter for any items that are not already dual-voltage.

EMERGENCIES

Medical centres

There are a few 24-hour tourist clinics in Denpasar and the Kuta area.
The first two have more advanced care for serious injuries.

International SOS Medical Clinic @ Jl Bypass Ngurah Rai 505X, Denpasar
🕓 (0361) 720 100

Bali International Medical Clinic @ Jl Bypass Ngurah Rai 100X, Denpasar
🕓 (0361) 761 263

Legian Clinic @ Jl Benesari, Legian 🕓 (0361) 758 503

CONSULATES & EMBASSIES

Australia ⓐ Jl Hayam Wuruk 88B, Denpasar ⓣ (0361) 241 118
ⓦ www.bali.indonesia.embassy.gov.au ⓔ bali.congen@dfat.gov.au
Canada/Ireland/New Zealand Contact the Australian consulate
South Africa ⓐ Jl Jend. Sudirman 28, Jakarta (on Java) ⓣ 021 574 0660
ⓔ saembcon@centrin.net.id
UK ⓐ Jl Tirta Nadi 20, Sanur ⓣ (0361) 270 601
ⓦ www.usembassyjakarta.org ⓔ bcbali@dps.centrin.net.id
USA ⓐ Jl Hayam Wuruk 188, Denpasar ⓣ (0361) 233 605
ⓦ www.britain.or.id ⓔ amcobali@indosat.net.id

GETTING AROUND

There's no rail service on Bali. Main roads run around the coasts and
generally north–south through the centre, following the ridges of the
central mountains.

EMERGENCY PHRASES

Help! Tolong saya! *Toe-long sigh-uh!*
Fire! Kebakaren! *Keh-bah-kah-ren!*
Stop! Estop! *Eh-stop!*
Call an ambulance/a doctor/the police! Panggilah ambulin/dokter/
polisi! *Pahn-gee-lah ahm-boo-leen/dok-ter/poh-lee-see!*
It's an emergency! Ini darurat! *Ee-nee dahr-oo-raht!*
I'm sick/injured. Saya sakit/terluka. *Sigh-uh sah-keet/teh-loo-kah.*
Where is a hospital/pharmacy? Dimana rumah sakit/apotek?
Dee-mahn-ah roo-mah sah-keet/ah-poh-tek?

EMERGENCY NUMBERS

Integrated Emergency Response Centre 112
Ambulance 118
Police 110
Fire 113

Car & motorcycle hire

Cars and motorcycles or scooters can be hired all over Bali; you'll see plenty of signs. Hertz (ⓦ www.hertz.com) and Avis (ⓦ www.avis.com) have offices on Bali, but charge at least six or seven times more than local places. Low-season prices will start at about Rp100,000 per day for cars and Rp50,000 per day for motorcycles, but you can always try negotiating (and enquire about insurance). Make sure you get a car suitable for your intended destination (e.g. 4-wheel drive for mountainous areas) and inspect the vehicle carefully first. The petrol tank will usually be empty, so you'll need to fill up at a service station as soon as you get it. Accidents are common here, especially for motorcycles (which should be ridden only by licensed, experienced drivers), so take special care or, better still, hire a private driver with his own car (see below).

C.V. Amertha Dana Car Rental ⓐ Pura Bagus Teruna #104, Legian ⓣ (0361) 753 518

Chartered transport

If you'd like to follow your own itinerary outside the main resorts, hiring a private driver with a vehicle can be the most hassle-free of methods, allowing you to leave the driving to someone else while you can enjoy the scenery and relax. A full day's hire should cost between Rp300,000 and Rp400,000 and include fuel; you can negotiate further with the driver for shorter trips. To find a driver just ask at your hotel or talk to the men on the street who will call out 'transport' and make a driving gesture as you walk by. Ask what they drive (usually a jeep or minivan) and whether it's air-conditioned, or try these drivers:

Wayan (Kuta) ⓣ (081) 239 612 96
Putu (Ubud) ⓣ (081) 338 741 541
Gede (Lovina) ⓣ (081) 239 829 41

Public transport

The most common form of transport for locals here are the colourful minivans known as *bemos*. They run along fixed routes (but with no real

DRIVING RULES & CONDITIONS

If you plan to drive here, you are required to have an International Driving Permit, obtainable from your country's motoring organisation if you're already licensed. (Be sure to carry your home licence as well.) This also applies for motorcycle licences. Traffic drives **on the left**. Driving conditions on Bali are, in a word, chaotic. Roads are infrequently maintained and can be smooth as silk or full of potholes and obstacles; traffic can consist of almost anything that moves, including cars, motorcycles, scooters, horsecarts, pedestrians and livestock. The busier tourist resorts and urban areas often have incredibly confusing one-way systems in place. Use your horn frequently to alert others of your presence, especially when going around blind turns. Developed areas have modern petrol stations; it's a good idea to fill up before heading out to the countryside. In rural areas, petrol (*bensin*) is sold in bottles by the roadside.

Speed limits are more of a concept than a rule here. Technically it's 96 km/h (60 mph) on country roads and the highway and 48 km/h (30 mph) on urban streets, but you should stick to traffic speed or slower for safety's sake – if you are involved in an accident, it will most likely be considered your fault as a foreigner.

Police here are not paid well and make it a practice to pull over foreign drivers for on-the-spot 'fines' for whatever infraction can be found (or made up), usually for Rp100,000. Say you don't have that much and offer between Rp20,000 and Rp50,000, making sure you hide your cash in a money belt beforehand so you have only a few small notes in your wallet to show.

timetables) and can be picked up from a terminal in larger towns or hailed from the road. Passengers call out at their stop and pay the driver upon disembarking. The fares are set by distance, but tourists can count on being charged more than locals, so you'll want to negotiate with the driver before you hop in. Make sure you have small change or notes with you (under Rp10,000) – it will be impossible to get change for anything larger. *Bemos* are cheap and found everywhere – they're especially handy for getting around more spread-out towns like Ubud – but they can be slow and uncomfortable and aren't suited for long trips with luggage (see below). Look out for pickpockets, too. Another option, often used late at night when the *bemos* have stopped running, are *ojeks* – motorbikes or scooters used to transport passengers (who ride pillion).

Taxis

Taxis are a fast, convenient and not terribly expensive way to get around the sprawling Kuta/Denpasar area, and your best option if you're going to or from Nusa Dua (no *bemos* run there) or travelling from Lombok's Gili Islands to the airport at Mataram. Look for the light blue 'Blue Bird' taxis, which have air-conditioned cars and English-speaking drivers. Tips are optional but it's customary to round up to the nearest Rp1,000 when paying.

Blue Bird Taksi ❶ (0361) 701 111 (Bali) ❶ (0370) 627 000 (Lombok)

Tourist transport

Perama, Bali's most reputable private transport company, operates daily shuttle buses for tourists from Kuta and the airport to Sanur, Ubud, Lovina, Padangbai and Candidasa, as well as chartered services to places like Amed, Bedugul and Tulamben. They're more expensive than *bemos* but well worth it, as they offer set timetables, shorter trips, more comfort and room for luggage, and even hotel pick-ups and drop-offs for an extra charge. They also run a tourist boat to the Gili Islands (see page 85) from Padangbai. Sample fares from Kuta (at time of writing): Sanur, Rp15,000; Ubud, Rp30,000; Padangbai/Candidasa, Rp40,000; Lovina, Rp85,000 to Rp100,000.

Perama ❶ (0361) 751 551 Ⓦ www.peramatour.com ❶ Booking a day ahead is recommended

Street names

Jalan is Indonesian for 'street' and is usually abbreviated as *Jl*. The 'correct' spelling of place and street names on Bali can vary, and some

roads are known by two names, official and colloquial (e.g. Jalan Arjuna is known as Jalan Double Six after a well-known nightclub).

HEALTH, SAFETY & CRIME
Health
Thankfully, most visitors to Bali have little to worry about beyond the annoyances of sunburn, mosquito bites and hangovers, but there are other potential issues to be aware of.

Malaria is not a risk in the resort areas of Bali, but **dengue fever** can be found on Bali and Lombok, and is carried by a different species of mosquito that bites during the day. Use insect repellent or wear long sleeves and trousers, especially if visiting inland or marshy areas, and if you experience fever, headache or joint and muscle pains after a bite, seek medical advice.

A number of **sexually transmitted diseases** are present on Bali, including HIV. You can purchase condoms from pharmacies, but it's best to bring your own.

Sunburn and dehydration are always a risk in tropical destinations. Wear high-SPF sunscreen (ideally with built-in insect repellent) daily and clothing to protect your skin. Be sure to drink plenty of (bottled) water during the day.

'Bali Belly' is the most common ailment for Western visitors. Do NOT drink the tap water on Bali – bottled water is both cheap and available, and should be used for brushing teeth, too. Ice in bars and restaurants is made from filtered water according to government regulations (but avoid it from street vendors). Be careful of spicy foods if you're not accustomed to them. Treat an upset stomach and diarrhoea with rehydration salts and anti-diarrhoea medicine, but consult a doctor if it lasts longer than a few days, becomes more severe or if a fever develops.

Western-quality health care can be found at a few tourist clinics in Denpasar, near Kuta (see **Emergencies**, page 115), but in other areas may be difficult to find outside some high-end hotels with doctors on staff. Bali's sole recompression chamber (for diving accidents) is located in the

Sanglah Public Hospital in Denpasar (ⓐ Jl Kesehatan Selatan 1
ⓣ (0361) 227 911). Pharmacies (*apotek*) are found in tourist areas and
cities, and sell a wide range of prescription and over-the-counter
medicines. There's a 24-hour *apotek* on Jalan Raya Seminyak, next door
to the Bintang Supermarket, in the northern end of the Kuta area.

Safety & crime
Violent crime isn't a worry on Bali, but as in most places, tourists should
take precautions against pickpockets and petty theft. Lock up your bags,
keep cash and passports hidden and secure, and don't put valuables in
a bum bag that can be easily snatched. Women travelling solo may
experience some harrassment from men in the Kuta area and on Gili
Trawangan during party nights, and it's a good idea to avoid dark alleys
and the beach late at night.

MEDIA
The main English-language newspapers are *The Jakarta Post*
(ⓦ www.thejakartapost.com) and *The Bali Times*
(ⓦ www.thebalitimes.com). *The Beat* (ⓦ www.beatmag.com) is a
free, biweekly entertainment guide to Bali that can be found all over
the Kuta area.

DRUGS
Indonesia imposes heavy penalties on the possession, trafficking
and use of illegal drugs, including imprisonment and death. Don't
buy drugs or agree to transport parcels for people you don't know
– it's not worth the risk. Foreign citizens are not immune from
Indonesian law, and in recent years more than a dozen unfortu-
nate Westerners have been imprisoned or received death
sentences for narcotics-related crimes in Bali.

OPENING HOURS

In busy tourist areas like Kuta, shops and restaurants will usually open early and close late to accommodate visitors, although in low season and in quieter resorts, shops will often shut earlier. Because time is more elastic here than in Western countries, set hours can vary, but generally speaking are as follows:

Banks 🕐 08.00–14.00 Mon–Thur; 08.00–12.00 Fri; occasionally 08.00–11.30 Sat

Businesses 🕐 08.00–16.00 Mon–Fri; 08.00–13.00 Sat

Shops 🕐 08.00–18.00 (later in tourist areas)

Restaurants 🕐 08.00–22.00 (later in tourist areas)

RELIGION

The overwhelming majority of Balinese are Hindu, and Bali is the only Hindu province in Indonesia, the world's largest Muslim country. Religious practice is an important part of Balinese life – every village has at least three temples, and there are estimated to be at least 20,000 of them on the island. You'll see small offerings to the gods laid out several times a day in front of shops, hotels and restaurants and in shrines and temples. Religious festivals are held frequently; enquire at your hotel or a local tourist office for a local schedule if you'd like to attend one (see **Customs**, page 115, for dress codes in temples).

TIME DIFFERENCES

Bali is on Central Indonesian Time, which is 8 hours ahead of the UK (GMT), 13 hours ahead of US Eastern Standard Time and 2 hours behind Australian Eastern Standard Time. Indonesia does not observe Daylight Saving Time.

TIPPING

High-end restaurants and hotels will usually include a 5–10% service charge along with the 11% tax (called 'plus-plus', they should be printed on your bill), so extra tipping is generally unnecessary in these cases. Smaller places like *warungs* don't add the 'plus-plus' and don't generally expect tips, although it's customary to round up bills to the nearest Rp1,000 when paying.

TOILETS

Public toilets are found infrequently on Bali; what you may find are likely to be Asian-style squat toilets without toilet paper. Tourist sights will sometimes have Western toilets with a collection box for donations towards upkeep. Restaurants and hotels all have Western toilets, and if you ask politely to use them you're unlikely to be refused.

TRAVELLERS WITH DISABILITIES

In general, Bali does not accommodate travellers with disabilities easily. Pavements can be quite rough and sometimes even broken, usually with high kerbs and no wheelchair ramps. There are no audible signals at pedestrian crossings. Many tourist sights, such as temples, require climbing steps. Many of the high-end hotels have accommodations in place for those with disabilities; be sure to enquire upon booking. It's also recommended to call airlines in advance to request assistance in embarking and disembarking at the airport.

⬥ *Life is at a leisurely pace on Bali*